WE TAKE YOUR
CONTRACTOR BUSINESS NEXT LEVEL

TENNESSEE

1 CONTRACTOR CLUB

The #1 Contractor Service Provider

Tennessee's #1 contracting school for over 15 years now offers expanded contractor services.

---

1 EXAM PREP
AMERICA'S #1 CONTRACTOR SCHOOL

Contractor Exam Prep

- ⊘ Live Virtual Classes
- ⊘ Online Courses & Tutoring
- ⊘ Exam Book Rental
- ⊘ Application Assistance

USE CODE **CLUB24**
FOR 10% OFF!

---

1 INSURANCE SOLUTIONS
AMERICA'S #1 CONTRACTOR INSURANCE

Contractor Insurance

- ⊘ General Liability Insurance
- ⊘ Builder's Risk Insurance
- ⊘ Workers' Compensation.
- ⊘ Life & Health Insurance

Scan Now
Get a Free Quote!

---

1 CONTRACTOR SOLUTIONS
AMERICA'S #1 CONTRACTOR SERVICES PROVIDER

Contractor Permits

- ⊘ Permit Expediters
- ⊘ General Trade Permits
- ⊘ License Registration
- ⊘ NOC Recording

USE CODE **PERMIT24**
50% OFF Your First Permit!

1ExamPrep.com
(877) 775-9400

1InsuranceSolutions.com
(877) 700-0243

1ContractorSolutions.com
(877) 702-5377

Author: One Exam Prep (1-877-804-3959)
www.1examprep.com

VISIT US HERE FOR EXCLUSIVE OFFERS

Unleashing the Power Of Digital Marketing For Your Contractor Business

- Company Branding
- Contractor Website
- Social Media Templates
- 1-on-1 Marketing Consultations
- Google Search Optimazation

WWW.154AGENCY.COM

TABLE OF CONTENTS

Below is the testing company information you will need concerning your exam.

For all state specific information please visit - PSI Exam License Page

1. Select Your State
2. Select TN Contractors
3. Select Your License Classification

Examination Outline

This examination is OPEN BOOK

Total Questions	40
% Required to Pass	72.5%
Time Allowed	130 Minutes

Subject Area	# of Questions
General Knowledge and Electrical Installation Requirements	7
Services, Feeders, and Branch Circuits	7
Overcurrent Protection	2
Grounding and Bonding	5
Conductors and Cables	4
Raceways and Boxes	5
Hazardous Locations, Special Occupancies, and Special Equipment	5
Low Voltage, Alarms, Signaling Systems, and Communications	2
Lighting, Signs, and General Use Equipment	3
Total Questions: 40	

Approved References

1. NFPA 70 - National Electrical Code, 2017
2. NFPA 70 - National Electrical Code Handbook, 2017
3. Code of Federal Regulations
4. NFPA 70E - Standard for Electrical Safety in the Workplace, 2012
5. Ugly's Electrical References

STRATEGY FOR TEST TAKING

The preparation for an exam starts at the beginning of the course. It is essential to have the subject's program, become aware of the program, know it, review the books and support materials, and attend classes or tutoring sessions. The greater the time invested in preparing for your exam,the more likely you will pass it the first time around. The exam is just the first goal of a long career.

Prepare Mentally and Physically

Preparing for the exams depends, to a large extent, on the way you study. But other factors directly influence your academic performance, such as diet and exercise. Although the idea is to maintain a healthy and balanced diet throughout the year and exercise regularly, it is even more essential when preparing for your exams.

It is about eating breakfast that gives us the energy to face the day and supply the brain with enough glucose to get the most out of our study hours. Hydrating correctly for the day with water, dividing meals into five or six, and not overdoing it with caffeine will enhance our ability to pay attention and improve memory.

The same thing happens with exercise: Exercising will help us remove stress, rest better, and wake up feeling refreshed and more alert. Regular exercise also improves learning on two levels: it boosts cognitive function and memory retention. The more oxygenated nutrients the brain gets, the better it can perform, especially during exams.

Study planning: The first step to successfully passing the exams is planning well. This involves studying the subjects or content areas that will be on the exam daily. As the day of the exam approaches, we will only have to do an in-depth review of the entire exam scope to reach the exam date with all the suitably prepared subjects.

Reading: It is the general way to get in touch with a topic. When reading the scope of the exam, we must identify different phases for reading comprehension. First, we must understand the text's ideas and then expose our doubts or convey to the instructor what we have not understood. After examining what we read, we will achieve a broad vision of the whole, and it will only be enough for us to look for the general ideas.

Highlighting the text: Highlighting will help us focus on the relevant information in the text, and later, will help us structure and organize for the actual exam. We will avoid overloading the text excessively with highlights, not to hinder the ability to find the right answers during the exam. Note: Most testing companies allow the references for open book exams to be highlighted and tabbed with permanently affixed tabs. Be sure to check with your State or Local Jurisdiction regarding your exam.

Organizational techniques: Organizing the study material is key to understanding the concepts that we have previously highlighted in the text. These techniques will help us clarify the subject's structure, order the ideas hierarchically, and shorten the text's length to facilitate review and active study.

Study sheets: Using study cards or flashcards may sound like a very old-fashioned technique, but it is quite an effective learning method for assimilating specific data. It is about making a 'mini summary' of an entire topic, which allows you to save a lot when creating them, and they are straightforward to consult.

Take Practice Tests: The practice tests are an excellent way to review before an exam; in addition to that, with these, you can check what you are failing and focus efforts where necessary. It is, without a doubt, one of the best study strategies!

How Can You Improve Your Exam Preparation?

Make sure:

- Study daily to make sure you understand the subject.
- Study each subject listed on the exam scope: highlight, make outlines, and summaries.
- When a topic is well learned, it is not easily forgotten. In studying the following topics, you will have to rely on the previous ones, serving as a review and consolidation.

- When the exam approaches, we have to review to anchor them more in memory.

How Can You Improve Taking the Exam?

- Losing the nerve before the exam: "nerves are useless and they are in the way of everything."
- Try to relax. Practice relaxation techniques.
- Do not try to check if you remember all the exam subjects; before the exam, your mind is in tension, you can no longer reinforce your memory, so concentrate on what you will do.
- Being physically and mentally fit: You must sleep well and get enough rest before the exam.
- Do not leave everything for the last moment; if you do, you give the memory time to settle the information it receives. The memory needs rest, and your memory will be more clear if there is order.

How Fully Understand the Exam Questions?

- Leave the nerves at home.
- Take your time to read the questions well. Read them all. Sometimes there may be more than one referring to the same topic, and you will have to decide the focus and content for each one.
- Before answering each particular question, read it several times until you make sure you understand it. Look for the keyword that tells you what to do: explain, demonstrate, define, calculate, find. If your exam is open book, look for keywords that will indicate which book to find the answer in — Practice Comprehensive Reading.
- After answering, reread the question and answers and double-check your selection.

How to Organize the Time You Have During the Exam?

- It is necessary to know each question's value since the same amount of time may not be devoted to each question or subject.
- Quick distribution of time is made. We must allow time for review.
- It would be best to start with the questions that you are familiar with and know the answers quickly. The best way to answer is by making, in the beginning, an outline that guides us during the exam.
- When there is no time to answer a question, don't leave the question not answered. It will be an automatic wrong answer rather than taking a 1 out of 4 chance of getting the answer correct.

How to Review and Correct the Exam?

- Before submitting the exam, you should review:

The content: Make sure that you have answered all the questions.

The form:

It is more than obvious to say that to pass any exam depends a lot on how you study, the time you dedicate, and the information retention capacity you have.

- However, it also requires taking into account many other factors, so the best we can do is use effective study techniques to help you pass that stressful exam.
- It is expected that as the exam approaches, nerves can begin to take over due to the lack of constant study. That is why it is essential to discover an ideal technique that will lead you to achieve success and pass.

Preparation to Examinations

As we previously mentioned, preparation for your exam starts at the beginning of the course. It is essential to have the subject's program, become aware of the program, know it, review the books and support materials, and attend classes or tutoring sessions. The more time invested in preparing for your exam, the more likely you will pass it the first time.

It is also essential to keep motivation high when studying and have a learning strategy for each subject. Above all, you should not fear exploring different study methods.

Conclusively, We Can Develop the Following Strategies

Method One:

You should not "jump" on the exam task immediately after you received it. It would also be best if you didn't go through the questions one at a time in their original order.

Observe the following procedure:

Read the directions very carefully. The exam instructions often contain valuable data. Always examine all guidelines carefully to make sure you understand what's being requested.

Take a deep breath, and then slowly scan your eyes throughout the exam to familiarize yourself with all the questions.

In the process, answer the questions to which you know the correct answer.

Tackle more difficult tasks, but don't spend too much time on them. Leave the most difficult questions for the end.

Your task is to give as many correct answers to questions that you are sure of. Scientists have proven that when you skim through the entire test, unresolved questions are already "looming" in your head even before seriously tackling its solution. This is very useful for a variety of reasons.

First, you subconsciously start thinking about a solution to the most challenging test questions.

Secondly, tests often come across questions containing hints and sometimes even a complete answer to other test questions.

In any case, before proceeding with the solution of exam tasks, first, review the questions and give answers where you can do it. Then start to puzzle over more complicated tasks.

Method Two:

Read each test question at least twice.

This is a handy tip because trick questions are widespread in tests. When we are in the exam, we want to solve the tasks as quickly as possible, as there is not enough time. Therefore, many students make a widespread mistake because they glimpse a question and immediately start sorting out the answers.

The fact is that test developers try to outwit the exam takers and dilute the standard tasks with tricky questions. Let's take a look at some of them:

In tests, you can often come across the following question: Which of the following does not contain "a," "b," or "c"? If you read the task inattentively, it is quite possible to quickly skip the "not" particle and give a wrong answer.

Other questions may contain several correct answers, and your task involves choosing the most correct one.

Summing up, you should not lose your vigilance since inattention often leads to mistakes. So, do not be lazy and reread the questions at least twice.

Method Three:

Double-check the answers right away, rather than postpone checking until the end.

The fact is that once you have answered the question, the information is still very fresh in your head. Therefore, by quickly checking your answers, you will significantly reduce the chances of accidentally missing one silly mistake. On the other hand, you will increase your chances of receiving a passing exam score.

However, this does not mean that you should not recheck your answers after solving all the tests. On the contrary, try to always leave some time for final checking. By adding this technique to your arsenal, you can undoubtedly increase the chance of getting a decent grade.

Method Four (for closed book exams):

If you come across a question, the answer to which you do not remember, or you feel that it literally "spins on the tongue" but does not come to mind, try to mentally transfer yourself to the place where you first heard about it.

There are 24 hours in a day. If 8 of them are spent sleeping, that gives you 16 hours to get some efficient and productive study done, right?

It seems simple enough. There are plenty of hours in a day, so why is it so hard to use this time effectively, especially around exam time?

We've found that managing their time effectively is one of the things that students struggle the most with around exam time. However, time management is also one of the things that schools never teach – how frustrating?!

In the weeks leading up to study leave, every teacher you have for every class you go to seems to pile on the work: Mrs Gibb from English class tells you that you have to prepare 3 practice essays for both your visual and written texts, your Geography teacher Miss Wood expects you to do every past exam paper for the last three years before the exam, Mr West your Maths teacher says that you have to finish all of the questions in that darned AME textbook if you want to do well on the exam.

But they expect you to do all of this without giving you any time management tips. Mrs Gibb, Miss Wood and Mr West all fail to tell you how it's humanly possible to complete all of this work without collapsing when you walk into the exam hall.

That's where we come in!

Read on for the time management tips that your teachers never gave you!

1. Focus on what you have to study – not what you don't.

It seems obvious, but think of all the times you've sat down to study and you've ended up spending 2 hours studying the concepts you already know like the back of your hand.

It's easier to study the subjects you like. Studying the concepts that you're already confident in is a lot less challenging than studying the concepts that you find the most difficult, as your brain will have to work less to learn this information.

Studying what you already know is a bad time management strategy because you'll leave all the important stuff to the last minute meaning you won't have the time to cover these concepts in depth.

The trouble with this tip is that it's often hard to decipher what you know and what you don't.

To figure out what you concepts you already know, and what concepts you still need to learn, complete a subject audit. A subject audit involves breaking down a particular subject into several points or sections and then analysing how well you know each of these points. You should spend most of your time studying those concepts that you have rated the most difficult. Find our study audit outline form here.

The key for effective time management is to review the easier material, but allow enough time to cover the harder concepts in depth so you're not left to study all of the most difficult concepts the night before the exam.

2. Work in sprints.

You may think that to have good time management skills you have to spend all of your time studying. However this is a misconception that many students hold.

Think of studying for exams like training for a marathon.

On your first day of training, you wouldn't go out and run 42kms. You would burn-out quickly due to a lack of prior training, and you would probably be put off running for a long time. This would not be a good way to manage your time. The better route to success would be to slowly work up to running the 42kms by running a bit further every day.

This simple idea of training in short bursts has been proven effective in all areas of human performance. You don't have to be a marathon runner to use this strategy!

When studying, you should start out small by studying in short, focused 'sprints' followed by brief breaks. Start by studying in 15 minute bursts followed by one 10 minute break. Over time, slowly increase the length of time you're studying (and breaking) for.

This strategy is effective because studying for short bursts promotes more intense focus, and will give your brain the time to process and consolidate information as opposed to studying for long periods of time which is not effective and may increase your chances of burnout.

Don't think of effective time management as studying for three hours straight with no breaks, think of effective time management as using your time wisely and in ways that will best promote retention of information.

Follow these steps to practice effective time management and become an expert studier (or marathon runner!) in no time:

1. **Set a timer for 15 minutes.**
2. **Put in some solid study until the timer goes off, making sure you're spending every minute working with no distractions.**
3. **Have a ten-minute break to check your phone, walk around, stretch, get outside etc.**
4. **Rinse and repeat.**
5. **Increase the amount of time you're studying for as you begin to feel more comfortable studying for extended lengths of time.**

3. Make a study system.

I'm sure you've been lectured by every teacher you've ever had to "make a study plan!!!" Study plans are effective for your time management, however they're sometimes hard to stick to.

Here at StudyTime, we find that the 'study system' is an effective strategy for really getting to the root of what you're studying. A study system is easier to stick to, and therefore fosters better time management skills, because it breaks tasks down into small chunks.

A study system is basically a simple list of steps that you can make to outline the steps you're going to take when you study. The list should start simple (4-5 things), but over time it should become more complex as you add steps to it.

Just like a workout plan at the gym or for sport, it will give you a clear direction of what action to take, making study much more efficient.

Over time, you can experiment with new study methods, and add them in to optimise the system.

Below is an example study formula that you could use when studying:

1. **Download the "Achievement Standard" from the NCEA website**
2. **Turn this into a checklist for what you already know and what you need to know**
3. **Break the checklist into main themes using a mind map**
4. **For each theme, make a summary sheet**
5. **After that, break down the key points of each summary and put these onto flash cards**
6. **Read through your notes and ensure you understand them, and then hit the flash cards**
7. **Test yourself on all of them first, then make two piles, one that's wrong and one that's right. Then redo the wrong pile again**
8. **Get someone else to test you**
9. **Practice exam papers – test yourself using exam papers from the past 2-3 years and time yourself**
10. **Work through the answers**
11. **Write a sheet of all tips/tricks i.e. things you got wrong in the practice exam papers**
12. **Redo exam paper and make model answers**
13. **Adjust flashcards if necessary i.e. make new ones based on the exam papers**
14. **Re-test all your flashcards**

Creating a study system will keep you on track and it will allow you to effectively plan out your time while studying.

Imagine your Maths teacher gave you seven equations to do for homework. How would you answer these questions? Would you do one question per day for seven days, or would you do all seven questions in one day?

You may think that it would be a better time management strategy to do all seven questions at once and get them over and done with. However, this is an ineffective way to manage your time.

The brain works better when it has time to process information. Neuroscience has shown that your brain needs time to consolidate information that has been newly learned, in order to form strong links between neurons and thus strong memories.

If the learning is done in one big chunk, you'll just forget it after three days. However, if you review it a day after, then you'll retain it for seven days.

When making a study schedule, you should space out when you study for each subject. For example, don't spend one day studying English, then the next day studying Maths, then the next day studying Biology. Instead, you should alternate studying for these subjects throughout the day. Do one hour of Maths, then one hour of English study, then one hour of Biology, and so on.

This is a much better way to manage your time, because the more often you review a concept, the more solidified it will be in your mind. This is because there will be more time to consolidate this into your memory. Also, taking breaks between reviewing certain concepts will give your brain time to process the information.

Try it out!

NFPA 70: National Electric Code 2017
Tabs and Highlights

These 1 Exam Prep Tabs are based on *NFPA 70: National Electrical Code, 2017.*

Each Tabs sheet has five rows of tabs. Start with the first tab at the first row at the top of the page and proceed down that row placing the tabs at the locations listed below. Place each tab in your book setting it down one notch until you get to the bottom of the page, and then start back at the top again. After you have completed tabbing your book (the last tab is usually the glossary, appendix, or index), then you may start highlighting your book.

This concludes the tabs for this book. Please continue with the highlights on the following page.

Section	Highlight
90.1	**Purpose: (A) Practical Safeguarding.** The purpose of this *Code* is the practical safeguarding of persons and property from hazards arising from the use of electricity.
90.2	**Scope: (A) Covered.** This *Code* covers the installation…for the following. Highlight (1) – (4). (B) **Not Covered.** This *Code* does not cover the following: Highlight (1) – (5).
90.4	**Enforcement.** This *Code* is intended to be suitable…and for use by insurance inspectors.
90.5	**Mandatory Rules, Permissive Rules, and Explanatory Material:** (A) **Mandatory Rules.** …characterized by the use of the terms *shall* or *shall not*.
90.7	**Examination of Equipment for Safety.** …examinations for safety made under standard conditions…determination through field inspections.
100	**Definitions: Scope.** Become familiar with all definitions essential to the application of this *Code*.
110.3	**Part I. General – Examination, Identification, Installation, Use, and Listing (Product Certification) of Equipment.** (A) **Examination:** Highlight (1) – (8).
110.5	**Conductors.** Conductors normally used to carry current shall be of copper or aluminum unless otherwise provided in the *Code*.
110.12	**Mechanical Execution of Work.** (A) **Unused Openings.** …shall be closed to afford protection substantially equivalent to the wall of the equipment.
110.13	**Mounting and Cooling of Equipment: (A) Mounting.** Wooden plugs driven into holes in masonry, concrete, plaster, or similar materials shall not be used.
110.14	**Electrical Connections.** Conductors of dissimilar metals shall not be intermixed in terminal… unless the device is identified for the purpose and conditions of use. (A) **Terminals.** …shall be made by means of pressure connectors…or splices to flexible leads. (B) **Splices.** Conductors shall be spliced or joined…or soldering with a fusible metal or alloy.
110.15	**High-Leg Marking.** …marked by an outer finish that is orange in color.
110.22	**Identification of Disconnecting Means**
110.26	**Part II. 1000 Volts, Nominal, or Less – Spaces About Electrical Equipment.** (1) **Depth of Working Space.** The depth of the working space in the direction of live parts shall not be less than that specified in Table 110.26 (A)(1). **Table 110.26(A)(1) Working Spaces**
110.31	**Part III. Over 1000 Volts, Nominal - Enclosure for Electrical Installations.** A fence shall not be less than…or more extension utilizing three or more strands of barbed wire or equivalent.

Section	Highlight
110.34	**Work Space and Guarding.**
	(A) **Working Space.** *Exception*: Where rear access is required to work on nonelectrical parts…a minimum working space of 30 in. horizontally shall be provided.
110.36	**Circuit Conductors.** Circuit conductors shall be permitted to be installed in raceways: in cable …conductors provided in 300.7, 300.39, 300.40, and 300.50.
110.54	**Part IV. Tunnel Installations over 1000 Volts, Nominal - Bonding and Equipment Grounding Conductors: (A) Grounded and Bonding.** …at intervals not exceeding 1000 ft throughout the tunnel.
	(B) **Equipment Grounding Conductors.** The grounding conductor shall be permitted to be insulated or bare.
110.75	**Part V. Manholes and Other Electrical Enclosures - Access to Manholes: (A) Dimensions.** Rectangular access openings…shall not be less than 26 in. in diameter.
200.6	**Means of Identifying Grounded Conductors.**
	(A) **Sizes 6 AWG or Smaller.** Highlight (1) – (8).
	(B) **Sizes 4 AWG or Larger.** Highlight (1) – (4).
	(D) **Grounded Conductors of Different Systems.** The means of identification shall be documented…where the conductor of different systems originate.
200.7	**Use of Installation of a White or Gray Color or with Three Continuous White or Gray Stripes.**
	(B) **Circuits Less Than 50 Volts.**
	(C) **Circuits of 50 Volts or More.** (2) A flexible cord having one conductor identified by a white …by a circuit that has a grounded conductor.
200.10	**Identification of Terminals: (A) Device Terminals.**
	(B) **Receptacles, Plugs and Connectors.**
	(1) Identification shall be by a metal or…the letter *W* located adjacent to the identified terminal.
200.11	**Polarity of Connections.** No grounded conductor shall be attached to any terminal or lead so as to reverse the designated polarity.
210.4	**Part I. General Provisions. Multiwire Branch Circuits: (A) General.**
	(B) **Disconnecting Means.**
210.5	**Identification for Branch Circuits: (B) Equipment Grounding Conductor.**
	(C) **Identification of Underground Conductors.**
210.6	**Branch-Circuit Voltage Limitations.**

Section	Highlight
	Table 220.56: Demand Factors for Kitchen Equipment – Other Than Dwelling Unit(s)
220.84	**Part IV. Optional Feeder and Service Load Calculations - Multifamily Dwelling.**
	(B) House Loads.
	(C) Calculated Loads. (3) The nameplate rating of the following: Highlight a – d.
	Table 220.84: Optional Calculations – Demand Factors for Three or More Multifamily Dwelling Units
	Table 220.88: Optional Method – Permitted Load Calculations for Service and Feeder Conductors for New Restaurants
225.6	**Part I. General – Conductor Size and Support.**
	(A) Overhead Spans. (1) For 1000 volts, nominal or less, 10 AWG copper or 8 AWG aluminum …longer span unless supported by a messenger wire.
225.7	**Lighting Equipment Installed Outdoors: (B) Common Neutral.**
225.18	**Clearance for Overhead Conductors and Cables.** Overhead spans of open conductor cables of not over 1000 volts, nominal, shall have a clearance of not less than the following:
	(1) 3.0 m (10 ft) (4) 5.5 m (18 ft)
225.51	**Part III. Over 1000 Volts - Isolating Switches.** Where oil switches or air, oil, vacuum, or sulfur …building disconnecting means.
230.2	**Part I. General – Number of Services: (B) Special Occupancies.** By special permission, additional services shall be permitted for either of the following: Highlight (1) – (2).
230.6	**Conductors Considered Outside the Building.** Under any of the following conditions:(1) – (5).
230.24	**Part II. Overhead Service Conductors – Clearances.**
	(A) Above Roofs. …not less than 2.5 m (8 ft) above the roof surface.
	(B) Vertical Clearance for Overhead Service Conductors.
	(1) 3.0 m (10 ft) at the electrical service entrance…does not exceed 150 volts to ground. (2) 3.7 m (12 ft)…does not exceed 300 volts to ground. (4) 5.5 m (18 ft)…such as cultivated, grazing, forest, and orchard.
230.50	**Part IV. Service-Entrance Conductors – Protection Against Physical Damage.**
	(A) Underground Service-Entrance Conductors.
230.51	**Mounting Supports: (A) Service-Entrance Cables.** …within 300 mm (12 in.) of every service …and at intervals not exceeding 750 mm (30 in.).
230.53	**Raceways to Drain.** shall be listed or approved.
230.71	**Part VI. Service Equipment – Disconnecting Means - Maximum Number of Disconnects:** **(A) General.** Highlight (1) – (4).

Section	Highlight
230.72	**Grouping of Disconnects: (A) General.** The two to six disconnects as permitted in 230.71 shall be grouped.
230.75	**Disconnection of Grounded Conductor.** Where the service disconnecting means does not disconnect the ground conductor from the premises wiring, other means shall be provided for this purpose in the service equipment.
230.82	**Equipment Connected to the Supply Side of Service Disconnect.** (5) Taps used only to supply …equipment and installed in accordance with requirements for service-entrance conductors.
230.91	**Part VII. Service Equipment – Overcurrent Protection - Location.** Where fuses are used as the service overcurrent device, the disconnecting means shall be located ahead of the supply side of the fuses.
230.95	**Ground-Fault Protection of Equipment.** …of more than 150 volts to ground not exceeding 1000 volts phase-to-phase for each service disconnector rated 1000 amperes or more.
230.202	**Part VIII. Services Exceeding 1000 Volts, Nominal - Service-Entrance Conductor.** **(A) Conductor Size.** Service-entrance conductors shall not be smaller than 6 AWG unless in multiconductor cable.
240.5	**Part I. General – Protection of Flexible Cords, Flexible Cables and Fixture Wires.** **(A) Ampacities.** **(B) Branch-Circuit Overcurrent Device.** **(2) Fixture Wire.** Highlight (1) – (6). **(4) Field Assembled Extension Cord Sets.** 20-ampere circuits – 16 AWG and larger
240.6	**Standard Ampere Ratings: (A) Fuses and Fixed-Tripped Circuit Breakers.** **Table 240.6 (A) Standard Ampere Ratings for Fuses and Inverse Time Circuit Breakers**
240.8	**Fuses or Circuit Breakers in Parallel.** Individual fuses, circuit breakers, or combinations thereof shall not otherwise be connected in parallel.
240.21	**Part II. Location - Location in Circuit: (B) Feeder Taps.** **(2) Taps Not over 7.5 m (25 ft) Long.** **(3) Taps Supplying a Transformer [Primary Plus Secondary Not over 7.5 m (25 ft) Long].**
240.24	**Location in or on Premises: (A) Accessibility.** **(D) Not in Vicinity of Easily Ignitable Material.**
240.51	**Part V. Plug Fuses, Fuseholders, and Adapters - Edison-Base Fuses: (A) Classification.** **(B) Replacement Only.**
240.83	**Part VII. Circuit Breakers - Marking: (C) Interrupting Rating.** …other than 5000 amperes. **(D) Used as Switches.**

25

NFPA 70E: Standard for Electrical Safety
in the Workplace, 2012
Tabs and Highlights

These 1 Exam Prep Tabs are based on *NFPA 70E: Standard for Electrical Safety in the Workplace, 2012.*

Each Tabs sheet has five rows of tabs. Start with the first tab at the first row at the top of the page and proceed down that row placing the tabs at the locations listed below. Place each tab in your book setting it down one notch until you get to the bottom of the page, and then start back at the top again. After you have completed tabbing your book (the last tab is usually the glossary, appendix, or index), then you may start highlighting your book.

*****This concludes the tabs for this book. Please continue with the highlights on the following page.*****

Section	Highlight
90.2(A)	**Covered.** This standard also includes safe work practices for employees performing other work activities that can expose them to electrical hazards as well as safe work practices for the following:
90.2(B)	**Not Covered.** This standard does not cover safety-related work practices for the following:
100	**I. General.** Highlight the following: - Accessible - Attachment plug - Bonded - Branch-circuit - Controller - Device - Exposed - Ground fault - Ground-fault service interrupter - Grounding conductor, equipment - Grounding electrode - Labeled - Luminaire - Overcurrent - Raceway - Receptacle - Switch, Isolating
110.2	**Training Requirements**
110.2(C)	**Emergency Procedures.** Training of employees in approved methods of resuscitation and automatic external defibrillator (AED) use, shall be certified by the employer annually.
110.2(D)(1)	**Qualified Person.** (Highlight entire paragraph).
110.2(D)(1)(f)	The employer shall determine, through regular supervision or through inspections conducted on at least an annual basis, that each employee is complying with safety-related work practices required by this standard.
110.2(D)(2)	**Unqualified Persons.** (Highlight entire paragraph).
110.2(D)(3)	**Retraining:** An employee shall receive additional training (or retraining) under any of the following conditions:

Section	Highlight
	Retraining shall be performed at intervals not to exceed 3 years.
110.2(E)	**Training Documentation.** The employer shall document that each employee has received the training required by 110.2.
	The documentation shall contain the content of the training, each employee's name, and dates of training.
110.3	**Electrical Safety Program**
110.3(E)	**Electrical Safety Program Procedures.** (Highlight entire paragraph).
110.3(G)	**Job Briefing**
110.3(G)(1)	Before starting each job, the employee shall conduct a job briefing with the employees involved.
110.3(H)	**Electrical Safety Auditing**
110.3(H)(1)	The frequency of the audit shall not exceed three years.
110.4	**Use of Equipment**
110.4(C)	**Ground-Fault Circuit-Interrupter (GFCI) Protection**
110.4(C)(2)	**Outdoors.** GFCI protection shall be provided when an employee is outdoors and operating or using a cord- and plug-connected equipment supplied by 125-volt, 15-, 20-, or 30-ampere circuits.
120.1	**Process of Achieving Electrically Safe Work Condition**
120.1(5)	Use an adequately rated voltage detector to test each phase conductor … Before and after each test, determine that the voltage detector is operating satisfactorily.
120.2	**De-energized Electrical Conductors or Circuit Parts That Have Lockout/Tagout Devices Applied**
120.2(C)(3)	**Audit procedures.** An audit shall be conducted at least annually.
120.2(D)(1)	**Simple/Lockout/Tagout Procedure:** Simple lockout/tagout plans shall not be required to be written for each application.
120.2(D)(2)	**Complex/Lockout/Tagout Procedure**
120.2(D)(2)(b)	All complex lockout/tagout procedures shall require a written plan of execution that identifies the person in charge.

Section	Highlight
120.2(F)	**Procedures.** The employer shall maintain a copy of the procedures required by this section and shall make the procedures available to all employees.
120.2(F)(2)	**Elements of Control.** The procedure shall identify the elements of control.
120.2(F)(2)(f)	Testing. The procedure shall establish the following:
120.2(F)(2)(f)(5)	Planning consideration that include methods of verification where there is no accessible exposed point to take voltage measurements.
130.1	**General.** (Highlight entire paragraph).
130.2	**Electrically Safe Working Conditions**
130.2(A)	**Energized Work**
130.2(A)(3)	**Less Than 50 Volts.** Energized electrical conductors and circuit parts that operate at less than 50 volts shall not be required to be de-energized … there will be no increased exposure to electrical burns or to explosion due to electric arcs.
130.2(B)	**Energized Electrical Work Permit**
130.4	**Approach Boundaries to Energized Electrical Conductors or Circuit Parts**
Table 130.4(C)(a)	**Approach Boundaries to Energized Electrical Conductors or Circuit Parts for Shock Protection for Alternating-Current Systems**
130.5	**Arch Flash Hazard Analysis.** The arch flash hazard analysis shall be updated when a major modification ore renovation takes place. It shall be reviewed periodically, not to exceed 5 years.
130.5(A)	**Arch Flash Boundary.** (Highlight entire paragraph).
130.5(C)	**Equipment Labeling.** (Highlight entire paragraph).
130.6(C)	**Illumination**
130.7	**Personal and Other Protective Equipment**
130.7(C)	**Personal Protective Equipment**
130.7(C)(7)	**Hand and Arm Protection**
130.7(C)(7)(a)	**Shock protection.** Employees shall wear rubber insulating gloves with leather protectors where there is danger of hand injury from electric shock due to contact with energized electrical conductors or circuit parts.

Section	Highlight
Table 130.7(C)(7)(c)	**Rubber Insulating Equipment, Maximum Test Intervals**
130.7(C)(9)	**Factors in Selection of Protective Clothing**
130.7(C)(9)(a)	Layering. Garments that are not arc rated shall not be permitted to be used to increase the arc rating of a garment or of a clothing system.
130.7(C)(11)	**Clothing material Characteristics.** Clothing consisting of fabrics, zipper tapes, and findings made from flammable synthetic materials that melt at temperatures below 600 F … shall not be used.
Table 130.7(C)(15)(a)	**Hazard/Risk category Classifications and Use of Rubber Insulating Gloves and Insulated and Insulating Hand Tools – Alternating Current Equipment**
Table 130.7(C)(15)(a)	Notes: (3) The use of "N" does not indicate that rubber insulating gloves and insulated and insulating hand tools are not required in all cases.
Table 130.7(C)(15)(b)	**Hazard/Risk category Classifications and Use of Rubber Insulating Gloves and Insulated and Insulating Hand Tools – Direct Current Equipment**
Table 130.7(F)	**Standards on Other Protective Equipment**
205.5	**Spaces About Electrical Equipment**
205.7	**Guarding of Energized Conductors and Circuit Parts**
205.9	**Clear Spaces**
205.10	**Identification of Components**
205.12	**Identification of Circuits**
210.3	**Conductors.** Current-carrying conductors (buses, switches, disconnects, joints, and terminations) and bracing shall be maintained to perform as follows: (1) – (2).
250.2	**Inspection and Testing of Protective Equipment and Protective Tools**
250.2(A)	**Visual.** Safety and protective equipment and protective tools shall be visually inspected for damage and defects … in no case shall the interval exceed 1 year.
Annex M	**Layering of Protective Clothing and Total System Arc Rating**
M.1	**Layering of Protective Clothing**
M.1.1	(Highlight entire paragraph).

29 CFR 1926 OSHA
Tabs and Highlights

These 1 Exam Prep Tabs are based on *29 CFR 1926 OSHA Construction Industry Regulations.*

Each Tabs sheet has five rows of tabs. Start with the first tab at the first row at the top of the page, and proceed down that row placing the tabs at the locations listed below. Place each tab in your book setting it down one notch until you get to the bottom of the page, and then start back at the top again. After you have completed tabbing your book (the last tab is usually the glossary, appendix, or index), then you may start highlighting your book.

*Note: Page numbers are not provided since the edition changes every six (6) months.

1 Exam Prep Tab	Section #
Table of Contents	ix
1903: Inspections, Citations	1903.3
Citations/Penalties	1903.14
1904: Recordkeeping Injuries	1904.0
Reporting Fatalities	1904.39
OSHA Forms	After 1904.46
Access to Records	1910.1020 (After 1926.33)
Noise Exposure	1926.52
Hazard Communications	1910.1200 (or 1926.59)
Personal and Life Saving Equipment	Subpart E
Respiratory Protection	1910.134
QFLT	1910.134(f)(6)
Fire Protection and Prevention	Subpart F
Yard Storage	1926.151(C)
Signs, Signals, and Barricades	Subpart G
Materials Handling, Storage, Use, and Disposal	Subpart H
Tools - Hand and Power	Subpart I
Compressed Air	1926.302(b)(4)
Welding and Cutting	Subpart J
Electrical	Subpart K

1 Exam Prep Tab	**Section #**
Scaffolds	Subpart L
Fall Protection	Subpart M
Roof Widths	1926.501 (b)(10)
Personal Fall Arrest Systems	1926.502(d)
Positioning Device Systems	1926.502(e)
Fall Protection Plan	1926.502(k)
Helicopters, Hoists, Elevators and Conveyors	Subpart N
Motor Vehicles	Subpart O
Excavations	Subpart P
Soil Classifications	Subpart P, Appendix A
Sloping and Benching	Subpart P, Appendix B
Demolition	Subpart T
Power Transmission and Distribution	Subpart V
Rollover & Overhead Protection	Subpart W
Stairways and Ladders	Subpart X
Diving	Subpart Y
Toxic and Hazardous Substances	Subpart Z
Cranes & Derricks in Construction	Subpart CC
1910: General Industry Standards	1910.12
Lockout/Tagout	1910.147
Glossary	Glossary
Index	Index

This concludes the tabs for this document. Please continue with the highlights below.

A.M. 03/16/2021

Section #	Highlight
1904.1(a)(1)	**Basic requirement:** If your company had ten 10 or fewer employees at all times during the last calendar year, you do not need to keep OSHA injury and illness records.
1904.7(b)(3)(i)	**General recording criteria:** *Do I count the day on which the injury…illness began?*
1904.7 (b)(3)(iv)	*How do I count weekends, holidays, or other days…work-related injury or illness.*
1904.7(b)(5)	*How do I record an injury or illness that involves medical treatment beyond first aid?*
1904.7(b)(5)(i)	*What is the definition of medical treatment?…does not include: Highlight (A) - (C).*
1904.7(b)(5)(ii)	*What is "first aid"? Highlight (b)(5)(ii)(A) through (b)(5)(ii)(N).*
1904.7 (b)(6)	*Is every work-related injury or illness case involving a loss of consciousness recordable? Yes, you must…regardless of the length of time the employee remains unconscious.*
1904.30(a)	**Multiple business establishments – Basic requirement:** You must keep a separate OSHA log for each establishment that is expected to be in operation for one year or longer.
1904.30(b)	**Implementation**
1904.30(b)(1)	*Do I need to keep OSHA injury and illness records for short-term establishments(…)? Yes, however, you do not have to…300 Log that covers all of your short-term establishments.*
1904.33(a)	**Retention and updating - Basic requirement:** You must save the OSHA 300 Log, the …301 Incident Report forms for five (5) years following the end of the calendar year.
1904.39(a)(1)	**Reporting fatalities, hospitalizations, amputations, and losses of an eye as a result of work-related incidents to OSHA:** Within eight (8) hours after the death of any employee… to the Occupational Safety and Health Administration (OSHA), U.S. Department of Labor.
1904.39(a)(2)	Within twenty-four (24) hours after the death of any employee…loss of an eye to OSHA.
1926.1	**Purpose and scope:** Highlight (a) and (b).
1926.3	**Inspections – right of entry:** Highlight (b).
1926.10(a)	**Scope of Subpart:** This Subpart contains the general rules of…Secretary by regulation.
1926.12(a)	**Reorganization Plan No. 14 of 1950 - General provisions:** Highlight all of (a).
1926.13	**Interpretation of statutory terms:** Highlight all of (c), (c)(1) and (c)(2).
1926.15(b)	**Relationship to the Services Contract Act; The Walsh-Healy Public Contracts Act:** The Walsh-Healy Public Contracts Act…engaged in the performance of said contract."
1926.16	**Rules of construction:** Highlight (a).
1926.20(a)(1)	**General safety and health provisions:** no contractor or subcontractor…health or safety.
1926.20(b)(1)	It shall be the responsibility of the employer…may be necessary to comply with this Part.
1926.21(b)(2)	**Safety training and education:** The employer shall…other exposure to illness or injury.
1926.26	**Illumination:** Highlight all.
1926.32(d)	**Definitions: Authorized person**

Section #	Highlight
1926.32(j)	**Definitions: Employee**
1926.32(m)	**Definitions: Qualified**
1926.32(n)	**Definitions: Safety factor**
1910.1020(e)(1)(i)	**Access to records - General:** Whenever an employee…within the fifteen (15) working of the reason for the delay and the earliest date when the record can be made available.
1926.50(d)(2)	**Medical services and first aid:** The contents of the first aid kit shall be placed in a…on each job and at least weekly on each job to ensure that the expended items are replaced.
1926.50	**Appendix A First Aid Kits:** (Nonmandatory) Highlight all.
1926.51(a)	**Sanitation - Potable water:** Highlight (a)(1) – (a)(6).
1926.51(c)(1)	**Table D-1** for number of employees and minimum number of facilities.
1926.52	**Occupational noise exposure: Table D-2–Permissible Noise Exposures**
1926.52(d)(2)(ii)	If the value of F_e exceeds unity (1) the exposure exceeds permissible levels.
1926.52(d)(2)(iii)	A sample computation showing an application of the formula in paragraph (d)(2)(ii) of… Since the value of F_e does not exceed unity, the exposure is within permissible limits.
1926.52(e)	Exposure to impulsive or impact noise should not exceed 140 dB peak sound pressure level.
1926.55	**Gases, vapors, fumes, dusts, and mists:** Review Appendix A – Threshold Limit Values of Airborne Contaminants for Construction.
1926.56	**Illumination: Table D-3 Minimum Illumination Intensities in Foot-Candles**
1926.57(b)	**Ventilation - Local exhaust ventilation**
1926.57(d)(2)	**Duration of operations:** Since dust capable of causing disability is, according to the… equipment should not remove same immediately until the atmosphere seems clear.
1926.57(f)(1)(vi)	**Clean air:** Air of such purity that it will not cause harm or discomfort to an individual if it is inhaled for extended periods of time.
1926.57(f)(2)(ii)	**Dust hazards from abrasive blasting:** The concentration of respirable dust…of this Part.
1926.57(f)(3)(i)	**Blast-cleaning enclosures:** Blast-cleaning enclosures shall be exhaust ventilated in such a way that a continuous inward flow of air will be maintained at all openings in the enclosure during the blasting operation.
1926.57(f)(5)(ii)	**Personal protective equipment:** Abrasive-blasting respirators shall be worn by abrasive-blasting operators: Highlight (A), (B), and (C).
1926.60	**Methylenedianiline – Scope and application:** (a)(1) This Section applies to all construction…including but not limited to the following: Highlight (i), (ii), (iii), and (iv).
1926.60(b)	**Definitions: 4,4' Methylenedianiline or MDA**
1926.60(c)	**Permissible exposure limits**

Section #	Highlight
1926.60(f)(1)(ii)	**Exposure monitoring:** Representative employee shall be determined on the basis of… shift for each job classification in each work area where exposure to MDA may occur.
1926.60(h)(5)(i)	**Compliance program:** The employer shall establish and implement a written program to reduce employee exposure to or below the PELs by means of engineering and work… (1) of this Section, and by use of respiratory protection where permitted under this Section.
1926.60(j)(2)(iv)	**Removal and storage:** MDA-contaminated work clothing or equipment shall be placed …and transported in sealed, impermeable bags, or other closed impermeable containers.
1926.60(l)(2)	**Signs and labels - Signs:** Highlight (l)(2)(i) thru (l)(2)(ii)(B)(2).
1926.60(n)(9)(vi)	**Medical removal protection benefits:** Voluntary removal or restriction of an employee. Where an employee, although not required by this Section to do so, removes an employee… benefits to the employee equal to that required by paragraph (n)(9)(v) of this Section.
1926.62(a)	**Lead - Scope:** Construction work is defined as work for construction, alteration and /or repair, including painting and decorating. It includes but is not limited to the following: Highlight: (a)(1) – (a)(7).
1926.62(c)(1)	**Permissible exposure limit:** The employer shall assure that no employee is exposed to lead at concentration greater than fifty micrograms per cubic meter of air (50 ug/m^3) averaged over an 8-hour period.
1926.62(d)(6)(ii)	**Frequency:** If the initial determination or subsequent determination reveals employee… for that employee except as otherwise provided in paragraph (d)(7) of this Section.
1926.62(f)(1)	**Respiratory protection - General:** the employer must provide employee an appropriate respirator that complies with the requirements of the paragraph. Respirators must be used during: Highlight (i) thru (iv).
1926.62(j)(2)	**Biological monitoring:** Highlight (j)(2)(i) – (j)(2)(i)(C).
1926.62(j)(2)(iv)	**Employee notification:** Highlight (j)(2)(iv)(A) and (B).
1926.65	**Appendix C 1. Occupational Safety and Health Program:** Highlight section.
1926.95(a)	**Criteria for personal protective equipment - Application:** Protective equipment, including personal protective equipment for eyes, face, head, and extremities, protective… the function of any part of the body through absorption, inhalation or physical contact.
1926.95(b)	**Employer-owned equipment:** Where employees provide their own protective equipment, the employer shall be responsible to assure its adequacy, including proper maintenance, and sanitation of such equipment.
1926.100	**Head protection:** Highlight all.
1926.102(a)(5)	**Eye and face protection:** Protectors shall meet the following requirements: (i) – (vi).
1910.134(b)	**Respiratory protection - Definitions: Escape-only respirator** means a respirator intended to be used only for emergency exits.
1910.134(f)(6)	QLFT may only be used to fit test negative pressure air purifying respirators that must achieve a fit factor of 100 or less.
1926.104	**Safety belts, lifelines, and lanyards:** Highlight (a) – (f).

Section #	Highlight
1926.105(c)(1)	**Safety nets:** Nets shall extend 8 feet beyond the edge of the work surface where employees …the work surface as practical but in no case more than 25 feet below such work surface.
1926.106	**Working over or near water:** Highlight (a) – (d).
1926.150(b)(1)	**Fire protection – Water supply:** A temporary or permanent water supply, of sufficient… equipment shall be made available as soon as combustible materials accumulate.
1926.150(c)(1)(vi)	**Portable firefighting equipment:** A fire extinguisher, rated not less than 10B, shall be provided…This requirement does not apply to the integral fuel tanks of motor vehicles.
1926.150(d)(2)	**Standpipes:** In all structures in which standpipes are required, or where standpipes… conspicuously marked. There shall be at least one standard hose outlet at each floor.
1926.151	**Fire prevention: Table F-1–Fire Extinguishers Data**
1926.151(c)(2)	**Open yard storage:** Driveways between and around combustible storage piles shall be… free from accumulation of rubbish, equipment, or other articles or materials. Driveways shall be so spaced that a maximum grid system unit of 50 feet x 150 feet is produced.
1926.152(d)(1)	**Flammable liquids – Fire control for flammable liquid storage:** At least one portable fire extinguisher…into any room used for storage of more than 60 gallons of flammable liquids.
1926.153	**Liquefied petroleum gas (LP-Gas):** Includes handling and storage as well as container. Specifications, **Table F-3** & **Table F-31** Storage of LP-gas.
1926.154	**Temporary heating devices: Table F-4**
1926.200(d)	**Accident prevention signs and tags – Exit signs:** Exit signs, when required, shall be lettered in legible red letters, not less than 6 inches high, on a white field and the principal stroke of the letters shall be at least three-fourths inch in width.
1926.200(h)(1)	**Accident prevention tags:** Accident prevention tags shall be used as a temporary means of warning employees of an existing hazard, such as defective tools, equipment, etc. They shall not be used in place of, or as a substitute for, accident prevention signs.
1926.250(b)	**General requirements for storage - Material storage:** Highlight (b)(1) thru (b)(7).
1926.251(a)(6)	**Rigging equipment and material handling – Inspections:** Each day before being used …warrant. Damaged or defective slings shall be immediately removed from service.
1926.251(d)	**Natural rope, and synthetic fiber:** Highlight (d)(1) and all of (d)(2) including (i) – (v).
1926.251(d)(3)	**Safe operating temperatures:** Highlight all.
1926.251	**Table H-1 Maximum Allowable Wear at any Point of Link**
	Table H-2 Number and Spacing of U-Bolt Wire Rope Clips
1926.252(a)	**Disposal of waste materials:** Whenever materials are dropped more than 20 feet to any point lying outside the exterior walls of the building, an enclosed chute of wood, or… closed in on all sides, through which material is moved from a high place to a lower one.
1926.300(b)(4)(iv)	**General requirements - Point of operation guarding:** The following are some of the machines which usually require point of operation guarding: Highlight (A) – (I).

Section #	Highlight
1926.300(d)(3)	**Switches:** All other hand-held powered tools, such as circular saws, chain saws, and… with a constant pressure switch that will shut off the power when the pressure is released.
1926.301	**Hand tools:** Highlight all.
1926.302(b)(3)	**Power-operated hand tools:** Highlight all.
1926.302(b)(4)	**Power-operated hand tools:** Highlight all.
1926.302(b)(6)	The use of hoses for hoisting or lowering tools shall not be permitted.
1926.303(b)(1)	**Abrasive wheels and tools - Guarding:** Grinding machines shall be equipped with safety… for the Use, Care and Protection of Abrasive Wheels, and paragraph (d) of this Section.
1926.303(c)(5)	**Use of abrasive wheels:** Highlight all.
1926.304(d)	**Woodworking tools – Guarding:** Highlight all.
1926.305(c)	**Jacks–lever and ratchet, screw, and hydraulic - Blocking:** Highlight all.
1926.350(a)(1)	**Gas welding and cutting - Transporting, moving, and storing compressed gas cylinders:** Valve protection caps shall be in place and secured.
1926.350(a)(10)	Oxygen cylinders in storage shall be separated from fuel-gas cylinders or combustible… barrier at least 5 feet high having a fire resistance rating of at least one-half hour.
1926.350(d)	**Use of fuel gas:** The employer shall thoroughly instruct employees in the safe use of fuel gas, as follows: Highlight all (d)(1) thru (d)(6).
1926.350(e)(2)	**Fuel gas and oxygen manifolds:** Fuel gas and oxygen manifolds shall be placed in safe, well ventilated, accessible locations. They shall not be located within enclosed spaces.
1926.351(d)	**Arc welding and cutting - Operating instructions:** Employers shall instruct employees in the safe means of arc welding and cutting as follows: Highlight (d)(1) thru (d)(5).
1926.354(a)	**Welding, cutting, and heating in way of preservation coatings:** Before welding cutting or heating is commenced on…made by a competent person to determine its flammability.
1926.403(i)(1)	**General requirements – Working space about electric equipment:** Highlight all.
1926.403(i)(1)(i)	**Working clearances:** Highlight all.
1926.403	**Table K-1 Working Clearances**
	Table K-2 Minimum Depth of Clear Working Space in Front of Electric Equip.
	Table K-3 Elevation of Unguarded Energized Parts Above Working Space
1926.404(b)(1)	**Branch circuits - Ground-fault protection:** Highlight (b)(1)(i) – (b)(1)(ii).
1926.404(b)(1)(iii)(E)	All required tests shall be performed: Highlight (E)(1) – (E)(4).
1926.404	**Table K-4 Receptacle Ratings for Various Size Circuits**
1926.405(a)(1)(ii)	**Wiring methods, components, and equipment for general use - Wiring in ducts:** Highlight all.
1926.405(j)	**Equipment for general use:** Highlight all (j)(1) thru (j)(1)(v).

Section #	Highlight
1926.405(j)(2)	**Receptacles, cord, connectors, and attachment plugs (caps):** Highlight thru (j)(2)(i) – (ii).
1926.407(a)	**Hazardous (classified) locations - Scope:** Highlight all.
1926.408(c)(4)	**Special systems - Equipment location:** Highlight all.
1926.450(b)	**Scope, application, and definitions applicable to this Subpart - Definitions:** Review
1926.451(a)	**General requirements - Capacity:** Highlight (a)(1), (a)(4), (a)(5), and (a)(6).
1926.451(b)	**Scaffold platform construction:** Highlight (b)(1) – (b)(5)(ii).
1926.451(c)(1)	**Criteria for supported scaffolds:** Supported scaffolds with height to base width (including outrigger supports, if used) ratio of more than four to one (4:1) shall be restrained from tipping by guying, tying, bracing, or equivalent means, as follows: Highlight (i) – (iii).
1926.451(d)(3)	**Criteria for suspension scaffolds:** Highlight all.
1926.451(d)(3)(viii)	Outrigger beams shall be placed perpendicular to its bearing support (usually the face beam may be placed at some other angle, provided the opposing angle tiebacks are used.
1926.451(e)	**Access:** Highlight (e) and (e)(1).
1926.451(e)(2)(v)	Hook-on and attachable ladders shall have a minimum rung length of 11 ½ inches; and
1926.451(e)(3)	Stairway-type ladders shall: Highlight (i) – (iv).
1926.451(g)(1)	**Fall protection:** Each employee on a scaffold more than 10 feet above a lower level shall be protected from falling to that lower level.
1926.451(g)(1)(iii)	**Fall protection:** Highlight all.
1926.451(g)(3)(ii)	**Fall protection:** Highlight all.
1926.451(g)(4)(vii)	**Fall protection:** Highlight all.
1926.451(h)(2)(ii)	**Falling object protection:** Highlight all.
1926.452	**Additional requirements applicable to specific types of scaffolds:** (a) **Pole scaffolds** (b) **Tube and coupler scaffolds** (c) **Fabricated frame scaffolds (tubular welded frame scaffolds)** (c)(6) Scaffolds over 125 feet in height above their base shall be…with such design. (d) **Plasterers', decorators', and large area scaffolds** (e) **Bricklayers' square scaffolds (squares)** (f) **Horse scaffolds** (g) **Form scaffolds and carpenters' bracket scaffolds** (h) **Roof bracket scaffolds** (i) **Outrigger scaffolds** (j) **Pump jack scaffold** (k) **Ladder jack scaffold** (1) **Window jack scaffold** (m) **Crawling boards (chicken ladders)** (n) **Step, platform, and trestle ladder scaffolds** (o) **Single-point adjustable suspension scaffolds**

Section #	Highlight
	(p) **Two-point adjustable suspension scaffolds (swing stages)**
	(q) **Multi-point adjustable suspension scaffolds, stonesetters'…, and masons'…**
	(r) **Catenary scaffolds**
	(s) **Float (ship) scaffolds**
	(t) **Interior hung scaffolds**
	(u) **Needle beam scaffolds**
	(v) **Multi-level suspended scaffolds**
	(w) **Mobile scaffolds**
	(x) **Repair bracket scaffolds**
	(y) **Stilts**
1926.453(b)	**Aerial lifts - Specific requirements - Ladder trucks and tower trucks:** Highlight (b)(1).
1926.454	**Training requirements:** Highlight all including (a) – (a)(5).
Appendix A	**Subpart L Appendix A Scaffold specifications:** *Note: This is indicating where more detail can be found for scaffolding which was defined above.* Highlight the two **Tables** under **1. Guidelines and Tables:** maximum intended nominal load (*this table correlates load with thickness for dressed and undressed lumber rated capacity*).
1926.500(b)	**Scope, application, and definitions applicable to this Subpart - Definitions:** Review.
1926.501(b)(1)	**Duty to have fall protection - Unprotected sides and edges:** Highlight all.
1926.501(b)(10)	**Roofing work on low-slope roofs:** Highlight all.
1926.501(b)(15)	**Walking/working surfaces not otherwise addressed:** Highlight all.
1926.501(c)	**Protection from falling objects:** When an employee is exposed to falling objects, the employer…hat and shall implement one of the following measures: Highlight (c)(1) – (c)(3).
1926.502(b)(1)	**Fall protection criteria and practices - Guardrail systems:** Highlight all.
1926.502(b)(2)	Highlight all.
1926.502(b)(2)(iv)	Highlight all.
1926.502(b)(3)	Highlight all.
1926.502(b)(4)	Highlight all.
1926.502(b)(9)	Highlight all.
1926.502(c)(1)	**Safety net systems:** Safety nets shall be installed as close as practicable under the walking …which employees are working, but in no case more than 30 feet (9.1 m) below such level.
1926.502(d)	**Personal fall arrest systems:** Highlight all.
1926.502(d)(9)	Lanyards and vertical lifelines shall have a minimum breaking strength of 5,000 pounds (22.2kN).
1926.502(d)(12)	Self-retracting lifelines and lanyards which do not limit free fall distance to 2 feet or less shall be capable of sustaining a minimum tensile load of 3,000 pounds…extended position.
1926.502(d)(15)	Anchorages used for attachment of personal fall arrest equipment shall be…being used to support or suspend platforms and capable of supporting at least 5,000 pounds (22.2 kN).

Section #	Highlight
1926.502(d)(16)	Personal fall arrest systems, when stopping a fall, shall: Highlight (16)(i) – (16)(v).
1926.502(e)(1)	**Positioning device systems:** Positioning devices shall be rigged such that an employee cannot free fall more than 2 feet.
1926.502(e)(2)	Positioning devices shall be secured to anchorage…3,000 pounds, whichever is greater.
1926.502(e)(5)	Connecting assemblies shall have a minimum tensile strength of 5,000 pounds.
1926.502(e)(6)	Dee-rings and snap hooks shall be proof-tested to a minimum tensile strength of 3600lbs. without cracking, breaking, or taking permanent deformation.
1926.502(f)(2)(i)	**Warning line systems:** The rope, wire, or chain shall be flagged at not more than 6-foot intervals with high-visibility material.
1926.502(f)(2)(ii)	The rope, wire, or chain shall be rigged and supported in such a way that its lowest point… surface and its highest point no more than 39 inches from the walking/working surface.
1926.502(f)(2)(iii)	After being erected, with the rope, wire, or chain attached, stanchions shall be capable… perpendicular to the warning line, and in the direction of the floor, roof, or platform edge.
1926.502(f)(2)(iv)	The rope, wire, or chain shall have a minimum tensile strength of 500 pounds (2.22 kN).
1926.502(g)	**Controlled access zones:** *This section defines storage areas, cover controls and stacking materials. Fall protection plan defined as option.* Highlight (g)(1) – (g)(5).
1926.502(k)	**Fall protection plan:** Highlight (k)(1) – (k)(10).
1926.552(b)(2)	**Material hoists, personnel hoists, and elevators:** All entrances of the hoistways shall …shall be painted with diagonal contrasting colors, such as black and yellow stripes.
1926.552(b)(2)(i)	Bars shall be not less than 2- by 4-inch wooden bars or the…than 42 inches above floor.
1926.552(c)(3)	**Personnel hoists:** Towers shall be anchored to the structure…not exceeding 25 feet.
1926.552(c)(14)(iii)	**Ropes:** Safety factors: **Minimum Factors of Safety for Suspension Wire Ropes**
1926.650(a)	**Scope, application and definitions applicable to this subsection - Scope and application:** This subpart applies to all open excavations made in the earth's surface. Excavations are defined to include trenches.
1926.650(b)	**Definitions applicable to this Subpart:** Review.
1926.651(c)(2)	**Means of egress from trench excavations:** A stairway, ladder, ramp or other safe means… 4 feet or more in depth so as to require no more than 25 feet of lateral travel for employees.
1926.651(g)(1)(i)	**Hazardous atmospheres – Testing and controls:** Where oxygen deficiency (atmospheres containing less than 19.5 percent oxygen) or a hazardous atmosphere exists or could reasonably be expected to exist, such as in excavations in landfill areas or excavations in areas where hazardous substances are stored nearby, the excavations greater than 4 feet in depth.
1926.651(i)	**Stability of adjacent structures**
1926.651(j)(2)	**Protection of employees from loose rock or soil:** Employees shall be protected from excavated or other materials or equipment that could pose a hazard by falling or rolling into …are sufficient to prevent materials or equipment from falling or rolling into excavations.

Section #	Highlight
1926.652(b)	**Requirements for protective systems - Design of sloping and benching systems**
1926.652(b)(1)	**Option (1)** Allowable configurations and slopes.
1926.652(b)(2)	**Option (2)** Determination of slopes and configurations using Appendices A and B.
1926.652(b)(3)	**Option (3)** Designs using other tabulated data.
1926.652(b)(4)	**Option (4)** Design by a registered professional engineer.
Subpart P(b)	**Appendix A Soil classification - Definitions: Submerged soil** means soil which is under water or is free seeping.
	Type A means cohesive soils with an unconfined compressive strength of 1.5 ton per square foot (tsf) (144 kPa) or greater. Examples of cohesive soils are: clay, silty clay, sandy clay, clay loam…considered Type A. However, no soil is Type A if: Highlight (i) – (v).
	Type B means: Highlight (i) – (vi).
	Type C means: Highlight (i) – (v).
Subpart P	**Appendix B Sloping and benching:** *This section provides pictorial descriptions of run to rise calculations. Also* **Figure B-1** *which relates the types of soil to the required run to rise (horizontal to vertical) ratio to determine the amount of slope.*
(b)	**Definitions: Distress** means that the soil is in a condition where a cave-in is imminent or is likely to occur. Distress is evidenced by such phenomena as the development of fissures in the face of adjacent to an open excavation; the subsidence of the edge of an excavation; the slumping of material from the face or the bulging.
(3)(ii)	**Actual Slope:** The actual slope shall be less steep than the maximum allowable slope, when there are signs of distress. If that situation occurs, the slope shall be cut back to an actual slope which is at least 1/2 horizontal to one vertical (1/2 H:1V) less steep than the maximum allowable slope.
(4)	**Configurations:** Configurations of sloping and benching systems shall be in accordance with Figure B-1.
	Highlight: **Figure B-1 Slope Configurations** and #3 under the Notes.
Subpart P	**Appendix C Timber shoring for trenches:** Tables **C-1.1** through **C-2.3**
Subpart P	**Appendix D Aluminum hydraulic shoring for trenches:** Tables **D-1.1** through **D-1.4** These are aluminum shoring components flow charts.
1926.700(b)	**Definitions applicable to this Subpart:** Highlight (b)(1) – (b)(9).
1926.702(b)	**Requirements for equipment and tools - Concrete mixers.** Concrete mixers with one cubic yard or larger loading skips shall be equipped with the following: (b)(1) – (b)(2).
1926.702(c)	**Power concrete trowels:** equipped with a control switch that will automatically shut off the power whenever the hands of the operator are removed from the equipment handles.
1926.702(j)	**Lockout/Tagout procedures**
1926.703(b)	**Shoring and reshoring**

Section #	Highlight
1926.706(a)	**Requirements for masonry construction:** A limited access zone shall be established… The limited access zone shall conform to the following: Highlight (a)(1) – (a)(5).
1926.706(b)	All masonry walls over 8 ft. in height shall be adequately braced to prevent overturning… shall remain in place until permanent supporting elements of the structure are in place.
1926.751	**Definitions:** Review.
1926.754	**Structural steel assembly**
1926.754(b)(2)	**The following additional requirements shall apply for multi-story structures:** At no time shall there be more than four floors or 48 feet…maintained as a result of the design.
1926.852(b)	**Chutes:** The openings shall not exceed 48 inches in height measured along the wall of the chute.
1926.859(b)	**Mechanical demolition:** The weight of the demolition ball shall not exceed 50 percent or the cranes rated load…line by which it is suspended, whichever results in a lesser value.
1926.968	**Definitions: Barricade** and **Barrier**
1926.1050(b)	**Definitions:** Review.
1926.1051(a)	**General requirements:** A stairway or ladder shall be provided at all…19 inches or more.
1926.1051(a)(2)	A double-cleated ladder or two or more separate ladders shall be provided when ladders… 25 or more employees, or when a ladder is to serve simultaneous two-way traffic.
1926.1052(a)(1)	**Stairways:** have landings of not less than 30 inches in the…and extend at least 22 inches.
1926.1052(a)(3)	Variations in riser height and tread depth shall not be over ¼-inch in any stairway system.
1926.1052(c)(1)	**Stairrails and handrails:** Stairways having four or more risers or rising more than 30… shall be equipped with: (i) At least one handrail; and (ii) One stair rail system along each unprotected side or edge.
1926.1052(c)(11)	Handrails that will not be permanent part of the structure being built shall have a minimum clearance of 3 inches…handrail and walls, stairrail systems, and other objects.
1926.1053(a)(1)	**Ladders:** Ladders shall be capable of supporting the following loads without failure: Highlight: (i) – (iii).

1926.1053(a)(3)(i)   Rungs, cleats, and steps of portable ladders and fixed ladders shall be spaced not less than 10 inches nor more than 14 inches apart.
1926.1053(a)(3)(ii) Rungs, cleats, and steps of step stools…not less than 8 inches apart, nor more than 12 inches as measured between center lines of the rungs, cleats, and steps.
1926.1053(a)(3)(iii)   Rungs, cleats, and steps of the base section of extension trestle ladders shall be not less as measured between center lines of the rungs, cleats, and steps.

1926.1053(a)(4)(i)	The minimum clear distance between sides of individual rung/step…shall be 16 inches.
1926.1053(a)(6)(i)	The rungs and steps of fixed metal ladders…otherwise treated to minimize slipping.
1926.1053(a)(7)	Ladders shall not be tied or fastened together…are specifically designed for such use.

Section #	Highlight

1926.1053(a)(8)   A metal spreader or locking device shall be provided on each stepladder to hold the front and back sections in an open position when the ladder is being used.

1926.1053(a)(13)   The minimum perpendicular clearance between fixed ladder rungs, cleats, and steps and... for which a minimum perpendicular clearance of 4½ inches (11 cm) is required.

1926.1053(a)(19) Where the total length of a climb equals or exceeds 24 feet...the following: (i) – (iii).

1926.1053(a)(21) Wells for fixed ladders shall conform to all of the following: (i) – (v).

1926.1053(a)(22) Ladder safety devices, and related...shall conform to all of the following: (i) – (iv).

1926.1053(a)(24) The side rails of a through or sidestep fixed ladders shall extend 42 inches above the top of the access level or landing platform...the access level shall be the top of the parapet.

1926.1053(b)(1)   **Use:** When portable ladders are used for access to an upper landing surface, the ladder side rails shall extend at least 3 feet...by itself, cause the ladder to slip off its support.

1926.1053(b)(5)(i) Non-self-supporting ...used at an angle such that the horizontal distance from the top support to the foot of the ladder is approx. one quarter the working length of the ladder.
1926.1053(b)(5)(ii) Wood job made ladders with spliced side rails shall be used at an angle that is one-eighth the working length of the ladder.

1926.1101(b)   **Asbestos - Definitions:** Review.

1926.1101(c)   **Permissible exposure limits (PELS)**

1926.1101(c)(1)   **Time-weighted average limit (TWA):** The employer shall ensure that no employee is exposed to an airborne concentration of asbestos in excess of 0.1 fiber per cubic centimeter of air as an eight-hour time-weighted average...or by an equivalent method.

1926.1101(g)(8)   **Additional Controls for Class II work:** Highlight all.

1926.1101(g)(8)(i)   For removing vinyl and asphalt flooring materials...these practices pursuant to paragraph (k)(9) of this Section: (i)(A) – (i)(I).

1926.1101(g)(8)(ii)   For removing roofing material which...following work practices are followed: (A) – (H).

1926.1101(g)(8)(iii)   When removing cementitious asbestos-containing siding and shingles or transite panels... the employer shall ensure that the following work practices are followed: (A) – (D).

1926.1101(g)(8)(iv)   When removing gaskets containing ACM...work practices are followed: (A) – (D).

1926.1101(g)(8)(v)   When performing any other Class II removal of asbestos containing material for which specific controls have not been...following work practices are complied with. (A) – (D).

1926.1101(g)(8)(vi)   **Alternative Work Practices and Controls:** Instead of the work practices and controls... the following provisions are complied with. (A) – (B).

1926.1101(h)(3)(ii) **Respirator protection:** Employers must provide an employee with tight-fitting, powered... the employee chooses to use a PAPR and it provides adequate protection to the employee.
1926.1101(h)(3)(iii)   Employers must provide employees with an air-purifying half mask respirator, other... whenever employees perform: Highlight (A) – (B).

NFPA 70E: Standard for Electrical Safety
in the Workplace, 2012
Questions and Answers

1. What is the frequency set by NFPA 70E for performing an audit of qualified persons working in your employ?

    A. Every 1 year
    B. Every 3 years
    C. Every 5 years
    D. Not required

2. GFCI protection shall be provided when an employee is outdoors and operating or using a cord- and plug connected equipment supplied by _____-volt, 15-, 20-, or 30-ampere circuits.

    A. 600
    B. 300
    C. 220
    D. 125

3. An employee shall receive retraining at intervals not to exceed _____ year(s).

    A. 1
    B. 3
    C. 5
    D. N/A, determined per the employers Electrical Safety Program

4. Clothing consisting of fabrics, zipper tapes, and findings made from flammable synthetic materials that melt at temperatures below _____ F shall not be used.

    A. 450
    B. 525
    C. 600
    D. 750

5. An employer's Electrical Safety Program shall be audited to verify it is in compliance with NFPA 70E at a frequency not exceed _____ year(s).

    A. 5
    B. 4
    C. 3
    D. 2

6. Energized electrical conductors and circuit parts that operate at less than ____ volts shall not be required to be de-energized and it is determined there will be no increased exposure to electrical burns or to explosion due to electric arcs.

    A. 300
    B. 125
    C. 50
    D. 25

7. Simple lockout/tagout plans _____.

    A. *shall* be required to be written for each application
    B. *shall not* be required to be written for each application
    C. *may* be required to be written for each application depending on the authority having jurisdiction
    D. *shall* be required to be written for each application for commercial properties

8. Which of the following are general safety-related maintenance requirements?

I. All working spaces about electrical equipment shall be maintained
II. Enclosures shall be maintained to guard against accidental contact with energized conductors
II. Access to working spaces shall be unobstructed
IV. Circuit or voltage identification shall be securely affixed and maintained in legible condition

    A. I and III
    B. I, II, and III
    C. II, III, and IV
    D. I, II, II and IV

9. Safety and protective equipment and protective tools shall be visually inspected for damage and defects before initial use and at intervals thereafter not to exceed a period of _____.

    A. 1 year
    B. 6 months
    C. 3 months
    D. 1 month

10. An energized work permit must be approved and signed by:

    A. Authorizing or responsible management
    B. Safety officer
    C. Owner
    D. Any of the above

11. The arc flash boundary for systems _____ volts and greater shall be the distance at which the incident energy equals 5 J/cm^2.

    A. 300
    B. 125
    C. 50
    D. 25

12. Electrical equipment such as panelboards that are in other than dwelling units and are likely to require maintenance while energized shall be marked with a label containing all of the following except _____.

    A. Nominal system voltage
    B. Danger – Energized Circuits
    C. Arc flash boundary
    D. Minimum arc rating of clothing

13. NFPA 70E covers safety-related work practices for _____.

    A. Installation of conductors that connect to the supply of electricity
    B. Installations of communications equipment under the control of communications utilities located outdoors
    C. Installation on properties leased or owned by the electric utility for the purpose of metering
    D. All of the above

14. Training of employees in approved methods of resuscitation and automatic external defibrillator (AED) use, shall be certified by the employer _____.

    A. Every 5 years
    B. Every 3 years
    C. Annually
    D. Quarterly

15. An arch flash hazard analysis shall be updated when a major modification or renovation takes place. It shall be reviewed periodically, not to exceed _____.

    A. 5
    B. 4
    C. 3
    D. 2

16. What is the shock protection limited approach boundary for a 300 volt energized exposed movable conductor?

    A. 3 ft. 6 in.
    B. 5 ft
    C. 10 ft
    D. 11 ft

17. What is the shock protection limited approach boundary for a 600 volt energized exposed movable conductor?

    A. 3 ft. 6 in.
    B. 5 ft
    C. 10 ft
    D. 11 ft

18. What is the restricted approach boundary for shock protection on 751 volt energized alternating current systems?

    A. 1 ft
    B. 2 ft. 2 in
    C. 3 ft. 3 in.
    D. 3 ft. 6 in.

19. What is the shock protection limited approach boundary for a 30 volt energized fixed circuit part?

    A. 3 ft. 3 in.
    B. 2 ft. 2 in
    C. 1 ft
    D. Not specified

20. Which of the following requires use of rubber insulating gloves?

   A. Circuit breaker (CB) or fused switch operation with covers on
   B. CB or fused operation with covers off
   C. Voltage testing on energized electrical conductors
   D. All of the above

Please see answer key of the following page

NFPA 70E: Standard for Electrical Safety
in the Workplace, 2012
Answers

1.	A	110.1(D)(1)(f)
2.	D	110.4(C)(2)
3.	B	110.2(D)(3)
4.	C	130.7(C)(11)
5.	C	110.3(H)(1)
6.	C	130.2(A)(3)
7.	B	120.2(D)(1)
8.	D	205.5, 205.7, 205.9, 205.12
9.	A	250.2(A)
10.	D	130.2(B)
11.	C	130.5(A)
12.	B	130.5(C)
13.	A	90(B)
14.	C	110.2(C)
15.	A	130.5
16.	C	Table 130.4(C)(a) and/or (b)
17.	C	Table 130.4(C)(a) and/or (b)
18.	B	Table 130.4(C)(a)
19.	D	Table 130.4(C)(a) and/or (b)
20.	C	Table 130.7(C)(15)(a)

Code of Federal Regulations (OSHA) 29 CFR 1926
Questions and Answers

1. The minimum distance between side rails for all portable ladders shall not be less than _____ inches.

    A. 11 ½
    B. 12
    C. 14
    D. 16

2. A stairway, ladder, ramp or other safe means of egress shall be located in trench excavations that are _____ feet or more in depth so as to require no more than _____ feet of lateral travel for employees.

    A. 4; 30
    B. 5; 30
    C. 4; 25
    D. 5; 25

3. Stairways that will not be a permanent part of the structure on which construction work is being performed shall have landings of not less than _____ inches in the direction of travel.

    A. 22
    B. 30
    C. 36
    D. 24

4. Toeboards, when used as falling object protection, shall be a minimum of _____ inches in vertical height.

    A. 3 ½
    B. 4
    C. 6
    D. 8

5. Scaffold fabricated planks and platforms shall be designed for a working load of _____ pounds per square foot (psf), if considered light duty.

    A. 15
    B. 20
    C. 25
    D. 50

6. A scaffold designed for 75 pounds per square foot (psf) is classified as _____.

   A. Light-duty
   B. Medium-duty
   C. Heavy-duty
   D. One-person

7. An extra-heavy-duty type 1A metal or plastic ladder shall sustain at least _____ times the maximum intended load.

   A. 2
   B. 2.5
   C. 4
   D. 3.3

8. A bricklayer's square scaffold load shall not exceed _____ pounds per square feet.

   A. 25
   B. 50
   C. 75
   D. 100

9. OSHA requires an employer to provide a training program for each employee _____.

   A. Using ladders and stairways
   B. Working with toxic substances
   C. Working in excavations
   D. Using scaffolding

10. Cord sets and receptacles which are fixed and not exposed to damage shall be tested at intervals not exceeding _____ months.

    A. 2
    B. 3
    C. 4
    D. 6

11. When portable ladders are used for access to an upper landing surface, the ladder side rails shall extend at least _____ feet above the upper landing surface to which the ladder is used to gain access.

    A. 3
    B. 4
    C. 5
    D. 6

12. Personnel hoistway doors or gates shall be not less than _____ high.

    A. 4 feet 6 inches
    B. 6 feet 6 inches
    C. 8 feet 6 inches
    D. None of the above

13. The minimum illumination for indoor corridors during construction shall be _____ foot-candles.

    A. 3
    B. 5
    C. 10
    D. 30

14. The span between hangers for plank-type platforms shall not exceed _____ feet.

    A. 6
    B. 8
    C. 10
    D. 12

15. Bricklayers square scaffolds shall not exceed _____ tiers in height.

    A. 2
    B. 3
    C. 4
    D. 5

16. Where toeboards are used for falling object protection, the toeboard shall be capable of withstanding, without failure, a force of at least _____ pounds applied in any downward or horizontal direction.

    A. 15
    B. 25
    C. 50
    D. 100

17. Fixed ladders without cages or wells shall have a clear width to the nearest permanent object of at least _____ inches on each side of the centerline of the ladder.

    A. 7
    B. 12
    C. 15
    D. 18

18. Rungs, cleats and steps of portable ladders (except for special applications such as stepstools) shall be spaced not less than _____ inches apart, nor more than _____ inches.

    A. 8; 11
    B. 9; 14
    C. 10; 14
    D. 12; 16

19. Wire rope shall not be used for material handling if in any length of _____ diameter(s) the total number of visible broken wires exceeds 10% of the total number of wires.

    A. 12
    B. 18
    C. 10
    D. 8

20. The minimum illumination of general construction area lighting is _____ foot-candles.

    A. 3
    B. 5
    C. 10
    D. 30

21. All new safety nets shall meet accepted performance standards of _____.

    A. 17,500 foot-pounds minimum impact resistance
    B. 24,000 foot-pounds minimum impact resistance
    C. Withstand five 200-pound sacks dropped simultaneously from a height of 25 feet
    D. 10,000-pound rope tensile strength

22. The contents of the first aid kit shall be placed in a weatherproof container with individual sealed packages for each type of item, and shall be checked by the employer before being sent out on each job and at least _____ on each job to ensure that the expended items are replaced.

    A. Daily
    B. Weekly
    C. Monthly
    D. Annually

23. If the personnel hoist wire rope speed is 300 feet per minute, the minimum rope safety factor must be _____.

    A. 9.20
    B. 9.50
    C. 9.75
    D. 10.00

24. The use of non-self-supporting ladders shall be at such an angle that the horizontal distance from the top support to the foot of the ladder is approximately _____ of the working length of the ladder.

    A. One-half
    B. One-quarter
    C. Three quarters
    D. Seven eighths

25. Stairs shall be installed between _____ and _____ degrees horizontal.

    A. 20; 40
    B. 20; 50
    C. 20; 30
    D. 30; 50

26. Each employee on walking/working surfaces shall be protected from falling through holes, including skylights, by covers capable of supporting, without failure _____ that may be imposed on the cover at any one time.

    A. At least twice the weight of employees, equipment and materials
    B. An 800-pound load
    C. A force of at least 200 pounds
    D. A force of at least 150 pounds

27. Class II hazardous locations are those that are hazardous because of the presence of _____.

    A. Combustible dust
    B. Ignitable fibers
    C. Flammable liquids
    D. Explosives

28. Combustible materials shall be piled with regard to the stability of the piles and in no case shall be higher than _____ feet.

    A. 12
    B. 14
    C. 16
    D. 20

29. OSHA requires that for a structural steel assembly, at no time shall there be more than _____ feet or _____ floors, whichever is less, of unfinished bolting or welding above the foundation.

    A. 20; 2
    B. 24; 2
    C. 30; 3
    D. 48; 4

30. The term "ROPS" means _____.

    A. Regional Operating Standards
    B. Required Operating Steps
    C. Rollover Protective Structures
    D. None of the above

31. The maximum allowable slope for Type A soil for a simple slope in an excavation of 20 feet or less in depth is _____.

    A. 1: 1
    B. 2: 1
    C. ½: 1
    D. ¾: 1

32. When employees are required to be in trenches of _____ feet or more, an adequate means of egress such as a ladder, stairway or ramp shall be provided.

    A. 3
    B. 4
    C. 5
    D. 6

33. Openings are defined as a gap or void _____.

    A. 12 inches or less in its least dimension in a floor
    B. 30 inches or more high and 18 inches or more wide in a wall
    C. Less than 12 inches but more than 1 inch in its least dimension in a floor
    D. 12 inches or more in its greatest dimension in a floor

34. The top edge height of top rails, or equivalent guardrail system members, shall be _____ inches.

    A. 30
    B. 36
    C. 42
    D. 48

35. The use of spiral stairways that will not be a permanent part of the structure on which construction work is being performed is _____.

    A. Permitted
    B. Prohibited
    C. Prohibited except with the permission of the building official
    D. Permitted if the stairway is at least 7 feet in diameter

36. One toilet shall be provided at the construction jobsite for a maximum of _____ employees.

    A. 5
    B. 10
    C. 15
    D. 20

37. A Class C fire is a fire caused by _____.

    A. Combustible metal
    B. Flammable liquid
    C. Trash
    D. Electrical equipment

38. When materials are dropped more than _____ feet outside the exterior walls of a building, an enclosed chute shall be used.

    A. 10
    B. 15
    C. 20
    D. 25

39. Material shall not be stored indoors within _____ inches of a fire door opening.

    A. 24
    B. 30
    C. 36
    D. 48

40. Scaffold planking that is nominal two inches thick shall be used for a _____ psf workload at a maximum span of _____ feet.

    A. 25; 10
    B. 50; 8
    C. 75; 6
    D. 25; 8

41. OSHA requires that a safety factor based on load and speed be used in hoist cables. The safety factor for a cable with a speed of 200 feet per minute is _____.

    A. 7.00
    B. 6.65
    C. 7.65
    D. 8.60

42. Safety belt lanyards used for employee safeguarding shall have a minimum breaking strength of _____ pounds.

    A. 1,000
    B. 4,000
    C. 5,000
    D. 5,400

43. The proper maintenance for a carbon dioxide type fire extinguisher is to _____.

    A. Discharge annually and recharge
    B. Check pressure gauge monthly
    C. Check pressure gauge annually
    D. Weigh semi-annually

44. No more than _____ gallons of flammable or combustible liquids shall be stored in a room outside of an approved storage cabinet.

    A. 10
    B. 15
    C. 20
    D. 25

45. Exposure to impulsive or impact noise shall not exceed _____ dBA peak sound pressure level.

    A. 92
    B. 110
    C. 140
    D. 188

46. Simple slope-short-term excavations in Type A soil with a maximum depth of 12 feet shall have a maximum allowable slope of _____.

    A. 1: 1
    B. 2: 1
    C. ¾: 1
    D. ½: 1

47. The ratio of the ultimate breaking strength of a piece of material or equipment to the actual working stress when in use is known as the _____.

    A. Occupational hazard
    B. Unstructibility
    C. Condition of protection
    D. Safety factor

48. Wire, synthetic or fiber rope used for scaffold suspension shall be capable of supporting at least _____ times the rated load.

    A. 6
    B. 4
    C. 3
    D. 2

49. The proper maintenance for a multi-purpose ABC dry chemical stored pressure fire extinguisher is to _____.

    A. Check pressure gauge monthly
    B. Discharge annually and recharge
    C. Weigh semi-annually
    D. Check pressure gauge and condition of dry chemical annually

50. Metal tubular frame scaffolds, including components such as braces, brackets, trusses, screws legs, ladders, etc. shall be designed, constructed and erected to safely support its own weight and at least _____ times the maximum intended load applied.

    A. 6
    B. 2
    C. 3
    D. 4

51. The maximum span of 2" x 10" undressed lumber on a scaffold when loaded with 50 psf shall be _____ feet.

    A. 5
    B. 6
    C. 10
    D. 8

52. On construction sites, a fire extinguisher rated not less than 2A shall be provided for each _____ square feet of the protected building area, or major fraction thereof.

    A. 1,000
    B. 2,000
    C. 3,000
    D. 4,000

53. Potable drinking water, per OSHA, requires that _____.

    A. If a container is used it shall be equipped with a tap
    B. A common drinking cup is allowed if washed
    C. Single serving cups do not have to be provided
    D. Open containers can be used if single serving cups are provided

54. A safety belt lanyard shall provide for a fall not greater than _____ feet.

    A. 3
    B. 6
    C. 12
    D. 15

55. The maximum allowable height of a horse scaffold shall be two tiers or _____ feet.

    A. 4
    B. 8
    C. 12
    D. 10

56. When using carpenters' bracket scaffolds, the _____.

    A. Brackets shall be spaced a maximum of 8 feet
    B. Bolts used to attach shall be not less than 5/8 inches in diameter
    C. Tools and materials shall not exceed 75 pounds
    D. All of the above

57. When a material hoist tower is not enclosed, the hoist platform shall _____.

    A. Be caged on all sides
    B. Have ½-inch mesh number 16 U.S. gage wire covering
    C. Have a five-foot enclosure at ground level
    D. All of the above

58. Employees cannot be subjected to noise levels higher than _____ dBA for more than four hours per day.

    A. 95
    B. 97
    C. 102
    D. 105

59. The range of maximum intended working loads for light to heavy-duty Independent Wood Pole Scaffolds shall be _____ pounds per square foot (psf).

    A. 20 – 75
    B. 25 – 70
    C. 25 – 75
    D. 25 – 50

60. Safety nets shall be provided when workplaces are more than _____ feet above the ground or water surface.

    A. 6
    B. 8
    C. 10
    D. 25

61. No more than _____ employee(s) shall occupy any given eight feet of a form scaffold at any one time.

    A. 1
    B. 2
    C. 3
    D. 4

62. Given the following: 1 ½ hours noise exposure at 90 dBA
                         ½ hour noise exposure at 100 dBA
                         ¼ hour noise exposure at 110 dBA

    If your employees are exposed to all of the above noise levels each workday, the "Equivalent Noise Exposure Factor _____.

    A. Exceeds unity, therefore the noise exposure is within permissible levels
    B. Exceeds unity, therefore the noise exposure is not within permissible levels
    C. Does not exceed unity, therefore the noise exposure is within permissible limits
    D. Does not exceed unity, therefore the noise exposure is not within permissible limits

63. A fire breaks out in a main electrical junction box at a construction site, an electrician is close by and asks you to get a fire extinguisher. According to OSHA, you should bring back a _____ extinguisher.

    A. Soda acid
    B. Foam
    C. Stored pressure (water type)
    D. CO_2

64. Oxygen cylinders, regulators and hoses shall be _____.

    A. Stored only in approved containers
    B. Prohibited in areas where fuel gasses other than acetylene are used
    C. Unpainted
    D. Kept away from oil or grease

65. A female employee complains that there are not separate toilets for the 20 women working on the site. She further states that all 160 employees use the same toilet. She said that the contractor is not complying with OSHA. According to the text, the employee _____.

    A. Does not have a valid complaint since OSHA has no specific instructions as to male and female toilets. The project is only required to have four toilets and four urinals
    B. Does not have a valid complaint since OSHA has no specific instructions as to male and female toilets. The project is only required to have five toilets and five urinals
    C. Has a valid complaint since OSHA specifies that five toilets and five urinals for men and a separate toilet for women are required on a project of that size
    D. Has a valid complaint since OSHA specifics four toilets and four urinals for men and a separate toilet for women are required on a project of that size

66. Employees shall not be exposed to noise levels exceeding _____ dBA for more than eight hours a day.

    A. 90
    B. 95
    C. 102
    D. 105

67. A Class A fire consists of burning _____.

    A. Wood
    B. Oil
    C. Electrical equipment
    D. Metals

68. Portable electric lighting used in wet and/or other conductive locations shall be operated at _____ volts or less.

    A. 12
    B. 32
    C. 110
    D. 220

69. _____ shall not be used if the rope shows other signs of excessive wear, corrosion, or defect.

    A. Alloy steel chains
    B. Synthetic fiber rope
    C. Natural rope
    D. Wire rope

70. According to OSHA, a sign lettered in legible red letters, not less than 6 inches high on a white field is used only as a/an _____ sign.

    A. Danger
    B. Exit
    C. Caution
    D. Safety Instructional

71. Material stored inside building under construction shall not be placed within _____ feet of any hoistway opening or inside floor openings.

    A. 4
    B. 5
    C. 6
    D. 10

72. Scaffold planks shall extend over the centerline of its supports at least _____ inches and not more than _____ inches.

    A. 6; 12
    B. 8; 12
    C. 9; 12
    D. 10; 16

73. A gap or void 2 inches or more in its least dimension in a floor, roof, or other walking/working surface is a _____.

    A. Toeboard
    B. Hole
    C. Breech
    D. Opening

74. Safety and health regulation for construction, the minimum diameter wire ropes used in personnel hoists shall be _____ inch.

    A. ½
    B. 5/8
    C. ¾
    D. 7/8

75. An electric power circular saw shall be _____.

    A. Equipped with constant pressure switch
    B. Equipped with a momentary on/off switch that may have a lock on control
    C. Equipped with a positive on/off control
    D. None of the above

76. For general cleaning operations, the compressed air shall be reduced to less than _____ psi.

    A. 100
    B. 20
    C. 25
    D. 30

77. For powder-actuated tools, fasteners shall be allowed to be driven into _____.

    A. Face brick
    B. Surface-hardened steel
    C. Cast iron
    D. None of the above

78. Sloping or benching for excavation more than _____ feet deep shall be designed by a registered professional engineer.

    A. 10
    B. 15
    C. 20
    D. 25

79. Stairway railings shall be capable of withstanding a minimum force of _____ pounds applied in any downward or outward direction at any point along the top edge.

    A. 100
    B. 150
    C. 200
    D. 250

80. Forms and shores in concrete shall not be removed until _____.

    A. Directed by the architect or engineer
    B. The removal time stated in the specifications has elapsed
    C. The concrete has attained the specified compressive strength
    D. The concrete has gained sufficient strength to support its weight and superimposed loads

81. When ropes are used to define controlled access zones, the rope shall have a minimum breaking strength of _____ pounds.

    A. 75
    B. 100
    C. 200
    D. 300

82. Excavations 8' or less in depth in Type A soil that have unsupported, vertically sided lower portions, shall have a maximum vertical side of _____ feet.

    A. 3
    B. 3.5
    C. 4
    D. 5

83. All the following are true concerning OSHA regulations about employees working over or near water except _____.

    A. Ring buoys with at least 90 feet of line shall be provided and readily available
    B. At least one lifesaving skiff shall be immediately available
    C. Where the danger of drowning exists, provide employees with life jackets or buoyant work vests
    D. At least one person certified in lifesaving swimming courses shall be employed at all times

84. _____ shall be located and determined prior to opening an excavation.

    A. Dump site
    B. Site entrances
    C. Underground installations
    D. Adjacent property elevations

85. The maximum intended load for a frame scaffold including its components is 1,000 pounds. The scaffold as described shall be designed to support a minimum of _____ ton(s).

    A. 1.0
    B. 1.5
    C. 2.0
    D. 4.0

86. Storing masonry blocks in stacks higher than 6 feet shall be permissible provided that _____.

    A. Bracing is installed at the 6-foot level
    B. Containment is provided every 4-foot
    C. The stack is tapered back one-half block per tier above the 6-foot level
    D. The stack is on a concrete floor

87. When hazardous waste cleanup and removal operations at any site take longer than _____ months to complete, the employer shall provide showers and changing rooms for employees exposed to such conditions.

    A. 3
    B. 6
    C. 9
    D. 12

88. No employee shall be exposed to lead at concentrations greater than _____ micrograms per cubic meter of air in an 8-hour period.

    A. 30
    B. 40
    C. 50
    D. 60

89. Training for Class II asbestos removal work requires hands-on training and shall take at least _____ hours.

    A. 2
    B. 8
    C. 12
    D. 16

90. Where oxygen deficiency (atmospheres containing less than 19.5 percent oxygen) or a hazardous atmosphere exists or could reasonably be expected to exist, such as in excavations in landfill areas or excavations in areas where hazardous substances are stored nearby, excavations deeper than _____ feet shall be tested before employees are allowed enter the excavation site.

    A. 3
    B. 4
    C. 5
    D. 6

91. Whenever a masonry wall is being constructed, a limited access zone shall be established. The access zone shall run the entire length of the wall, on the side of the wall that is not scaffolded and extend to the height of the wall to be _____.

    A. Reconstructed
    B. Reconstructed plus two feet
    C. Reconstructed plus four feet
    D. Reconstructed plus six feet

92. An employer shall ensure that no employee is exposed to an airborne concentration of asbestos in excess of _____ fiber(s) per cubic centimeter of air as averaged over a 30-minute sampling period.

    A. 1.0
    B. 2.0
    C. 10.0
    D. 20.0

93. A wire core manila rope is used as a lifeline where it may be subjected to cutting or abrasion. The required minimum size of the rope shall be _____ inch.

    A. 1/2
    B. 3/4
    C. 7/8
    D. 1

94. Routine inspection of open excavations shall be conducted by a competent person _____.

    A. Daily
    B. Weekly
    C. Every two days
    D. Every three days

95. Haulage vehicles, whose payload is loaded by means of cranes, power shovels, loaders, or similar equipment, shall have _____.

    A. Pneumatic tires capable of supporting 1-1/2 times the payload capacity
    B. Automatic dumping mechanisms capable of payload leveling
    C. An automatic transmission and a cab shield on the load side of the operator station
    D. A cab shield and/or canopy adequate to protect the operator from shifting or falling materials

96. When removing hazardous waste materials, personal protection equipment is divided into four categories based upon protection required. _____ has the highest level of respiratory protection but a lesser level of skin protection.

    A. Level A
    B. Level B
    C. Level C
    D. Level D

97. Fuel gas and oxygen manifolds shall NOT be placed _____.

    A. Indirect sunlight
    B. No closer than 15' of main electric
    C. Elevated at least 6' off of a dirt floor
    D. They shall not be located within enclosed areas

98. The term "point of operation" refers to the _____.

    A. Starting point of a project
    B. Specific operation of a project being performed
    C. Area of a project where work is underway
    D. Area on a machine where work is actually performed\

99. For excavation made in Type C soil, the minimum, above the top of the vertical side, that the support shield systems at the vertically sided lower portion of an excavation be shielded or supported shall be _____ inches.

    A. 20
    B. 18
    C. 16
    D. 14

100. The highest stack allowed when bricks are being stored shall be _____ feet.

    A. 5
    B. 7
    C. 9
    D. 10

101. Employees shall be provided with anti-laser eye protection devices when working in areas in which a potential exposure to reflected laser light is greater than _____ milliwatts.

    A. 5
    B. 4
    C. 3
    D. 2

102. The minimum illumination required for first aid stations shall be _____ foot-candles.

    A. 30
    B. 20
    C. 5
    D. 3

103. A job site having 90 employees with temporary restrooms shall have a minimum of _____ toilets and urinals.

    A. One toilet and one urinal
    B. Two toilets and two urinals
    C. Three toilets and three urinals
    D. Four toilets and four urinals

104. Employees shall be protected from excavated or other materials or equipment that could pose a hazard by falling or rolling into excavations. The minimum distance required from the edge of excavations for placing and keeping such materials or equipment is _____ feet.

    A. 2
    B. 3
    C. 4
    D. 5

105. Not more than _____ gallons of Category 4 flammable liquids shall be stored in any one storage cabinet.

    A. 25
    B. 60
    C. 80
    D. 120

106. A hand-held grinder with a 2-1/8" diameter wheel shall be equipped with only a _____.

    A. Constant pressure switch
    B. Momentary contact on/off switch
    C. Positive percussion switch
    D. Positive on/off switch

107. Each end of a scaffold platform, unless cleated or otherwise restrained, shall extend over the centerline of its support at least _____ inches.

    A. 2
    B. 4
    C. 6
    D. 12

108. Where scaffold platforms are overlapped to create a long platform, platforms shall be secured from movement or overlapped at least _____ inches unless the platforms are nailed together or otherwise restrained to prevent movement.

    A. 2
    B. 4
    C. 6
    D. 12

109. When lifting concrete slabs, operation of jacks shall be synchronized in such a manner as to insure even and uniform lifting of the slab. All points of the slab support shall be kept level within _____ inches.

    A. 1/2
    B. 1
    C. 1-1/2
    D. 2

110. A "Controlled Access Zone" is implemented to protect employees from access to an area where the erection of precast concrete members is being performed. The control lines in a "Controlled Access Zone" shall be erected not more than _____ feet from the unprotected or leading edge or half of the length of the member being erected, whichever is less.

    A. 6
    B. 15
    C. 25
    D. 60

111. Shoring for concrete shall be designed by a _____.

    A. Contractor
    B. Carpenter
    C. Qualified designer
    D. Lumber supplier

112. All masonry walls over _____ feet in height shall be adequately braced to prevent overturning and to prevent collapse unless the wall is adequately supported so that it will not overturn or collapse.

    A. 8
    B. 12
    C. 16
    D. 20

113. Self-supporting portable ladders shall be capable of supporting without failure at least _____ times the maximum intended load.

    A. 3
    B. 4
    C. 5
    D. 6

114. A non-self-supporting ladder has a working length of 20'. According to OSHA, the horizontal distance from the top support to the foot of the ladder is approximately _____ foot/feet.

    A. 1/4 of a
    B. 4
    C. 5
    D. 6

115. During asbestos removal, the asbestos disposal contractor shall erect _____ rooms in the decontamination area.

    A. 2
    B. 3
    C. 4
    D. 5

116. All pneumatic nailers, staplers and other similar equipment provided with automatic fastener feed shall have a safety device to prevent the tool from ejecting fasteners when operation pressures exceed _____ psi.

    A. 75
    B. 100
    C. 125
    D. 150

117. A portable ladder that is NOT self-supporting must be capable of supports at least _____ times the maximum intended load.

    A. 2
    B. 4
    C. 6
    D. 8

118. The common drinking cup is _____.

    A. Prohibited
    B. Not prohibited
    C. Prohibited in areas where more than 3 workmen will use the cup
    D. Prohibited in hazardous areas

119. Eye protection near dangerous working conditions _____.

    A. Is required at the employee's cost
    B. Is required at the employer's cost
    C. Can only be required by union regulations
    D. Is not required

120. During construction, the minimum illumination required for an indoor warehouse shall be _____ foot- candles.

    A. 3
    B. 5
    C. 10
    D. 30

121. When safety nets are required to be provided, such nets shall extend _____ feet beyond the edge of the work's surface.

    A. 4
    B. 6
    C. 8
    D. 10

122. The mesh size of safety nets shall not exceed _____.

    A. 12" x 12"
    B. 10" x 10"
    C. 8" x 8"
    D. 6" x 6"

123. When masonry blocks are stacked higher than _____ feet, the stack shall be tapered back one-half block per tier above the six-foot level.

    A. 4
    B. 6
    C. 8
    D. 10

124. Lumber that is handled manually shall not be stacked more than _____ feet high.

    A. 14
    B. 16
    C. 18
    D. 20

125. The components of a scaffold loaded with 500 pounds shall be capable of supporting its own weight and a load of at least _____ ton(s) without failure.

    A. 1
    B. 2
    C. 2.5
    D. 4

126. All site clearing equipment shall be equipped with an overhead and rear canopy guard of at least 1/8" steel plate or _____ inch woven wire mesh with openings no greater than one inch, or equivalent.

    A. 1/8
    B. 1/4
    C. 3/8
    D. 1/2

127. Where doors or gates open directly on a stairway, a platform shall be provided, and the swing of the door shall not reduce the effective width of the platform to less than _____ inches.

    A. 16
    B. 18
    C. 20
    D. 24

128. Cohesive soil packed with an unconfined compressive strength of less than 1.5 tons per square foot but greater than .5 tons per square foot is defined as _____.

    A. Type A
    B. Type B
    C. Type C
    D. Type D

129. A six-foot deep trench excavated in Type C soil shall have the sides sloped at a maximum of _____.

    A. ¾:1
    B. 1:1
    C. 1 ½ : 1
    D. 1 ½: 1 ½

130. A simple slope excavation with a depth of 10 feet and which will be open for 20 hours shall have a maximum allowable slope of _____ in Type A soil.

    A. 1: ¾
    B. ¾ : 1
    C. 1: ½
    D. ½ : 1

131. When Type C soil is excavated over Type A soil, Type A soil shall be excavated to a maximum slope of _____ in layered soils.

    A. 1: ¾
    B. 1:1
    C. ¾ : 1
    D. 1 ½ : 1

132. Lifting inserts that are embedded, or otherwise attached to precast concrete members, other than the tilt-up members, shall be capable of supporting at least _____ times the intended maximum load.

    A. 2
    B. 3
    C. 4
    D. 5

133. The maximum number of manually controlled jacks allowed for lift-slab construction operations shall be limited to _____ on one slab.

    A. 8
    B. 10
    C. 12
    D. 14

134. The approximate angle of repose for sloping the sides of an excavation, less than 20' deep, in sand shall be _____.

    A. 90°
    B. 53°
    C. 45°
    D. 34°

135. When excavating in the proximity of adjoining buildings, a general contractor shall _____ for the safety and protection of workers.

    A. Remove all loose soils and rocks
    B. Compact adjacent soils and slope walls
    C. Provide adequate shoring and bracing systems
    D. Request a variance to move excavation farther away

136. When single post shores are tiered, they shall _____.

    A. Never be spliced
    B. Be vertically aligned
    C. Be designed by a licensed engineer
    D. Be adequately braced at top and bottom

137. When erecting systems-engineered metal buildings, during placing of rigid frame members, the load is not to be released from the hoisting equipment until _____.

    A. The crane operator signals that is safe to proceed
    B. All bolts have been installed and tightened to the specified torque
    C. The members are secured with not less than 50% of the required bolts at each connection
    D. Drift pins have driven into at least two bolt holes at each connection for the member

138. Prior to site layout, the contractor shall _____.

    A. Obtain a certificate of occupancy and provide proof of occupancy
    B. Alert subcontractors to the requirements of their scope
    C. Start erecting structural steel and roof support members
    D. Locate surface encumbrances that may pose a hazard to employees

139. Drawings or plans, including all revisions, for concrete formwork (including shoring equipment) shall be available at the _____.

   A. Jobsite
   B. Owner's office
   C. Contractor's main office
   D. Building department's office

140. Shoring for supported concrete slabs shall be removed only when the contractor _____.

   A. Has had it inspected by the building inspector
   B. Makes sure the concrete is dry to the touch
   C. Determines that the concrete has gained sufficient strength to support its weight and superimposed loads
   D. Has been told by the concrete supervisor that it is safe to strip the shoring

141. Where electrical transmission lines are energized and rated at least 50 kW or less, a minimum clearance distance of _____ feet shall be maintained.

   A. 5
   B. 8
   C. 10
   D. 12

142. When debris is dropped through a hole in the floor without the use of chute, the drop area shall be enclosed with barricades measuring a minimum of _____ inches.

   A. 30
   B. 36
   C. 42
   D. 48

143. _____ require "point of operation guarding."

   A. Hand chisels
   B. Guillotine cutters
   C. Powder-actuated tools
   D. 1 ½ inch abrasive wheel grinder

144. A _____ scaffold has an adjustable platform mounted on an independent support frame and is equipped with a means to permit platform raising or lowering.

   A. Multi-point adjustable suspension
   B. Single-point adjustable suspension
   C. Two-point adjustable suspension
   D. Masons' adjustable supported

145. At more than _____ feet above a lower level, the tubular welded frame scaffolding shall have approved guardrails and toe boards at all open sides and ends.

    A. 4
    B. 6
    C. 10
    D. 12

146. A minimum of _____ bolts shall be in place at each structural steel beam connection during final placing of solid web members before the load is released.

    A. One
    B. Two
    C. Three
    D. Four

147. The maximum allowable height, without being retrained from tipping, for a free-standing mobile scaffold tower that has a base width of 4 feet is _____ feet.

    A. 12
    B. 16
    C. 20
    D. 24

148. The minimum plywood thickness required for an overhead protective covering above a material or personnel hoist cage is _____ inch(es).

    A. 5/8
    B. ¾
    C. 7/8
    D. ½

149. The maximum permissible span for a 2" x 9" full thickness undressed lumber scaffold plank, when used for a light duty rated load is _____ feet.

    A. 6
    B. 8
    C. 9
    D. 10

150. The maximum intended load on a float or ship scaffold shall be _____ lbs.

    A. 250
    B. 500
    C. 750
    D. 1,000

151. Which of the following is true about electric power-operated tools furnished by the contractor,

    A. Each tool shall be cleaned daily after use
    B. Each tool shall be checked daily before use
    C. Each tool shall be tested daily before use
    D. Each tool shall be double insulated or grounded

152. A _____ is an accidental failure of a cross brace in an excavation.

    A. Kickout
    B. Slip-in
    C. Workout
    D. Cave-in

153. The maximum permissible span for 1 ¼ x 9-inch full thickness wood plank having a maximum intended load of 50 pounds per square foot is _____ feet.

    A. 4
    B. 6
    C. 8
    D. 10

154. The minimum breaking strength for vertical lifelines used for fall protection shall be _____ pounds.

    A. 3,000
    B. 4,000
    C. 5,000
    D. 5,400

155. _____ gauge U.S. standard wire is used for the screen between the toe boards and top rails of an approved guardrail system.

    A. No. 12
    B. No. 14
    C. No. 16
    D. No. 18

156. A ground fault circuit interrupter, GFCI, which is not a part of the permanent wiring of the building on a construction site, protects the _____.

    A. Cord sets
    B. Power tools
    C. Personnel
    D. Wiring

157. The maximum opening size permitted in the ¼" woven wire mesh, used as a rear canopy guard on rider-operated equipment, when used for site clearing shall be _____ inch.

    A. 1
    B. ¾
    C. ½
    D. ¼

158. When a contractor discovers a piece of machinery on site which is not in compliance with OSHA requirements the contractor should _____.

    A. Physically remove the machinery from the site
    B. Identify the problem and inform anyone who operates it
    C. Only operate the machinery on weekend or holidays
    D. Schedule service to remedy the problem within 48 hours

159. A general contractor is building an apartment building with two exterior balconies. The general contractor and the carpentry subcontractor sign an agreement where the carpentry subcontractors will provide all temporary railings. There are 3 other subcontractors and their employees working on the site, using the balconies, when an OSHA inspector arrived and found the railing to be inadequate and unsafe. Which of the following represents the most likely outcome of this inspection visit?

    A. The general contractor and all subcontractors on site will be fined the full amount
    B. Only the carpentry subcontractor will be fined the full amount
    C. Only the general contractor can be fined on the project
    D. Only the general and the carpentry subcontractor will be fined

160. Of the following, which is not a true statement per OSHA regulations?

    A. Jobsite first-aid kits shall be checked by the employer daily
    B. Common drinking cups are prohibited for potable water
    C. A jobsite with 50 employees must have 2 toilets and 2 urinals
    D. The maximum duration of exposure to a sound level of 92 dba is 6 hours

161. According to OSHA, a hazardous atmosphere containing less than _____ percent oxygen may exist in deep excavations.

    A. 100
    B. 75
    C. 50
    D. 19.5

162. Which of the following is a true statement concerning OSHA regulations?

    A. Manually stacked lumber piles shall not be more than 16 feet in height
    B. Material stored inside building may not be placed within 2 feet of doors
    C. Brick stacks shall not be more than 6 feet in height
    D. Masonry blocks shall not be stacked more than 7 feet in height

163. Employers shall not issue or permit the use of unsafe hand tools. Which of the following tools is considered unsafe?

    A. A drift pin with a mushroomed head
    B. A splintered wooden handled shovel
    C. A pipe wrench with a sprung jaw
    D. All of the above are unsafe tools

164. Powder-actuated tools shall be tested _____ to insure proper working condition.

    A. Every hour of each day in use
    B. Each day before loading
    C. One per week
    D. After a malfunction occurs

165. "Asbestos containing material" is any material that contains _____ asbestos.

    A. Up to one percent
    B. More than one percent
    C. Two percent or less
    D. Between five and seven percent

166. Guarding for use with belts, gears, shafts, pulleys, drums, fly wheels or other power operated tools with reciprocating, rotating or moving parts should meet the requirements of _____.

    A. OSHA Regulations
    B. American National Standards Institute
    C. Florida Building Code
    D. U.S. Department of Labor

167. In excavations where a trench shield system is installed, the maximum depth of earth material that can be excavated below the bottom of the shield is _____ inches.

    A. Zero
    B. Not more than 6
    C. Not more than 12
    D. Not more than 24

168. In accordance with OSHA, the _____ has the responsibility of being safe, conducting activities safely and in accordance with all applicable laws and rules.

    A. Individual
    B. Employer
    C. Building official
    D. Foreman

169. The minimum number of sanitation facilities (chemical toilets) required for a 10-person mobile crew having transportation readily available to nearby toilet facilities is _____.

   A. Not less than 1 toilet
   B. 2
   C. 3
   D. Zero

170. _____ soil, which looks and feels damp, can easily be shaped into a ball and rolled into small diameter threads before crumbling.

   A. Cohesive
   B. Fissured
   C. Moist
   D. Granular

171. Inspections of alloy steel chains when used for rigging equipment for material handling shall occur _____.

   A. Daily
   B. Weekly
   C. Monthly
   D. Annually

172. Concrete mixers with _____ or larger loading skips shall be equipped with guardrails installed on each side of the skip.

   A. One cubic foot
   B. Ten cubic feet
   C. One cubic yard
   D. Ten cubic yards

173. A dry chemical, sodium or potassium bicarbonate-based fire extinguisher operated by cartridge is ranked as a type _____ extinguisher.

   A. A
   B. B
   C. C
   D. B and C only

174. When using control lines to demarcate controlled decking zones, non-mandatory guidelines require that each line be rigged and supported in such a way that its highest point is not more than _____ inches from the working surface.

   A. 39
   B. 40
   C. 42
   D. 45

175. A powder-operated tool shall be tested _____.

    A. Each day before loading
    B. Once a week
    C. Once a month
    D. At least semi-annually

176. A room used for storage of more than 60 gallons of flammable or combustible liquids shall have at least one portable fire extinguisher, having a rating of not less than 20-B units, shall be located outside of, but nor more than _____ feet from the door opening into the room.

    A. 5
    B. 7
    C. 10
    D. 12

177. The maximum number of people that can use a ladder jack scaffold at the same time is _____.

    A. 1
    B. 2
    C. 3
    D. 4

178. Guardrail systems shall be designed capable of withstanding a force of at least _____ pounds.

    A. 100
    B. 150
    C. 200
    D. 250

179. Toeboards are required on scaffolding more than _____ feet in height.

    A. 6
    B. 8
    C. 10
    D. 3

180. All pneumatically driven nailers provided with automatic fastener feed, which operate at more than 100 psi pressure at the tool shall have a _____.

    A. Slight angle to the decking
    B. Safety device installed at the muzzle
    C. Regulated pressure to not exceed 110 psi
    D. Regulated pressure not to have less than 90 psi

181. When using a hand-tool that is not grounded, the user should make sure the tool is _____.

    A. Double insulated
    B. Dust free
    C. Newly painted
    D. Serviced by a three-prong adapter

182. Each employee on a scaffold more than _____ feet above a lower level must be protected from falling to that lower level.

    A. 6
    B. 8
    C. 10
    D. 12

183. Scaffolding cannot be moved with employees still on it unless the surface on which it is moving is within _____ degrees of level.

    A. 2
    B. 3
    C. 4
    D. 5

184. Material chutes at an angle of more than 45° from the horizontal shall have openings not to exceed _____ inches in height.

    A. 24
    B. 48
    C. 60
    D. 72

185. When it is not practical to use nails to secure roof bracket scaffolds, brackets shall be secured in place with first-grade manila rope of at least _____ inch(es).

    A. ½
    B. ¾
    C. 1
    D. 1 ½

186. The warning line erected around all sides of the roof work area shall not be less than _____ feet from the roof edge when mechanical equipment is not being used.

    A. 3
    B. 4
    C. 5
    D. 6

187. On low-sloped roofs of _____ feet or less in width, the use of a safety monitoring system alone as a means of providing fall protection during roofing operation is permitted.

    A. 40
    B. 45
    C. 50
    D. 60

*** *Please see Answer Key on the following page* ***

OSHA Federal Safety and Health Regulations
Questions and Answers
Answer Key

Q	Answer	Section #
1.	A	1926.1053 (a)(4)(ii)
2.	C	1926.651 (c)(2)
3.	B	1926.1052 (a)(1)
4.	A	1926.502 (j)(3)
5.	C	Subpart L, Appendix A 1(c)
6.	C	Subpart L, Appendix A 1(c)
7.	D	1926.1053 (a)(1)(i)
8.	B	Subpart L, Appendix A 2(e)
9.	A	1926.1060 (a)
10.	D	1926.404 (b)(1)(iii)(E)(4)
11.	A	1926.1053 (b)(1)
12.	B	1926.552 (c)(4)
13.	B	1926.56, Table D-3
14.	C	Subpart L, Appendix A 2(p)(4)
15.	B	1926.452 (e)(4)
16.	C	1926.451(h)(4)(i)
17.	C	1926.1053 (a)(17)
18.	C	1926.1053 (a)(3)(i)
19.	D	1926.251 (c)(4)(iv)
20.	B	1926.56, Table D-3
21.	A	1926.105 (d)
22.	B	1926.50 (d)(2)
23.	A	1926.552 (c)(14)(iii)
24.	B	1926.1053 (b)(5)(i)
25.	D	1926.1052 (a)(2)
26.	A	1926.501 (b)(4)(ii) & 1926.502(i)(2)
27.	A	1926.449
28.	D	1926.151 (c)(1)

Q	Answer	Section #
29.	D	1926.754 (b)(2)
30.	C	1926.1002
31.	D	Subpart P, Appendix B, Table B-1 Maximum Allowable Slopes
32.	B	1926.651 (c)(2)
33.	B	See "Opening" in Glossary or 1926.500(b)
34.	C	1926.502 (b)(1)
35.	B	1926.1051 (a)(1)
36.	D	1926.51, Table D-1
37.	D	Subpart F, Table F-1 – Fire Extinguishers Data
38.	C	1926.252 (a)
39.	C	1926.151 (d)(7)
40.	D	Subpart L, Appendix A, Scaffold Specifications, (1)(b)(i), Table
41.	D	1926.552 (c)(14)(iii)
42.	D	1926.104 (d)
43.	D	Subpart F, Table F-1 – Fire Extinguishers Data
44.	D	1926.152 (b)(1)
45.	C	1926.52 (e)
46.	D	Subpart P, Appendix B, Table B-1 Maximum Allowable Slopes Figure B-1 Slope Configurations Figure B-1.1 Excavations made in Type A Soil
47.	D	See "Safety Factor" in Glossary or 1926.32(n)
48.	A	1926.451 (a)(4)
49.	D	Subpart F, Table F-1 – Fire Extinguishers Data
50.	D	1926.451 (a)(1)
51.	D	Subpart L, Appendix A (1)(b)(i), Table
52.	C	1926.150 (c)(1)(i)
53.	A	1926.51 (a)(2)
54.	B	1926.104 (d)
55.	D	1926.452 (f)(1)
56.	D	Subpart L, Appendix A, Scaffold Specifications, Paragraph (g)(2)(3)(4)
57.	A	1926.552 (b)(5)(ii)
58.	A	1926.52, Table D-2

Q	Answer	Section #
59.	C	Subpart L, Appendix A, Scaffold Specifications, 2. Specifications and Tables, (a) Pole Scaffolds, Table: Independent Wood Pole Scaffolds
60.	D	1926.105 (a)
61.	B	Subpart L, Appendix A, Scaffold Specifications, 2.Specific Guidelines and Tables (g)(4)
62.	C	1926.52 (d)(2)(iii) $Fe = (T1 \div L1) + (T2 \div L2) + (Tn \div Ln)$ $Fe = (1/4 \div \frac{1}{2}) + (1/2 \div 2) + (1\frac{1}{2} \div 8)$ $Fe = 0.500 + 0.25 + 0.188$ $Fe = 0.938$
63.	D	Subpart F, Table F-1 – Fire Extinguishers Data
64.	D	1926.350 (i)
65.	A	1926.51, Table D-1
66.	A	1926.52 (d)(1), Table D-2
67.	A	Subpart F, Table F-1 – Fire Extinguishers Data
68.	A	1926.405 (a)(2)(ii)(G)
69.	D	1926.251 (c)(4)(iv)
70.	B	1926.200 (d)
71.	C	1926.250 (b)(1)
72.	A	1926.451 (b)(4) & (5)
73.	B	See "Hole" in Glossary or 1926.500(b)
74.	A	1926.552 (c)(14)(ii)
75.	A	1926.300 (d)(3)
76.	D	1926.302 (b)(4)
77.	D	1926.302 (e)(7)
78.	C	Subpart P, Appendix B, Table B-1 Maximum Allowable Slopes (Note 3)
79.	C	1926.1052 (c)(5)
80.	D	1926.703 (e)(2)
81.	C	1926.502 (g)(3)(iii)
82.	B	1926.652, Subpart P Appendix B, Figure B-1 Slope Configurations B-1.1 Excavations made in Type A soil
83.	D	1926.106
84.	C	1926.651(b)(1)
85.	C	1926.451(a)(1) $1,000 \times 4 = 4,000$ $4,000 \div 2,000 = 2$ tons

Q	Answer	Section #
86.	C	1926.250(b)(7)
87.	B	1926.65 (n)(7)
88.	C	1926.62 (c)(1)
89.	B	1926.1101 (k)(9)(iv)(A)
90.	B	1926.651(g)(1)(i)
91.	C	1926.706(a)(2)
92.	A	1926.1101(c)(2)
93.	C	1926.104(c)
94.	A	1926.651(k)(1)
95.	D	1926.601(b)(6)
96.	B	1926.65 Appendix B, Part A, II
97.	D	1926.350(e)(2)
98.	D	1926.300(b)(4)(i)
99.	B	1926.652 Subpart P Appendix B, Figure B-1 Slope Configurations Figure B-1.3 Excavations Made in Type C Soil
100.	B	1926.250(b)(6)
101.	A	1926.54(c)
102.	A	1926.56, Table D-3 Minimum Illumination Intensities in Foot-Candles
103.	C	1926.51, Table D-1
104.	A	1926.651(j)(2)
105.	D	1926.152(b)(3)
106.	B	1926.300(d)(2)
107.	C	1926.451(b)(4)
108.	D	1926.451(b)(7)
109.	A	1926.705(g)
110.	D	1926.502(g)(1)(ii)
111.	C	1926.703 (b)(8)(i)
112.	A	1926.706(b)
113.	B	1926.1053(a)(1)(i)
114.	C	1926.1053(b)(5)(i) 20 feet ÷ 4 feet = 5 feet
115.	B	1926.1101(j)(1)(i)
116.	B	1926.302(b)(3)

Q	Answer	Section #
117.	B	1926.1053(a)(1)(ii)
118.	A	1926.51(a)(4)
119.	B	1926.102(a)(1)
120.	B	1926.56, Table D-3 Minimum Illumination Intensities in Foot-Candles
121.	C	1926.105(c)(1)
122.	D	1926.105(d)
123.	B	1926.250(b)(7)
124.	B	1926.250(b)(8)(iv)
125.	A	1926.451(a)(1)
		500 x 4 = 2,000 = 1 ton
126.	B	1926.604(a)(2)(i)
127.	C	1926.1052(a)(4)
128.	B	1926.652, Subpart P Appendix A (b)
129.	C	1926.652, Subpart P Appendix B, Table B-1 Maximum Allowable Slopes
130.	D	1926.652, Subpart P Appendix B, Figure B-1.1 Excavations made in Type A soil
131.	C	1926.652, Subpart P Appendix B, Figure B-1.4 Excavations Made in Layered Soils
132.	C	1926.704(c)
133.	D	1926.705(j)
134.	D	1926.652 Subpart P Appendix A (b) Note: "Sand" is classified as Type C soil 1926.652 Subpart P Appendix B, Table B-1 Maximum Allowable Slopes
135.	C	1926.651(i)(1)
136.	B	1926.703(b)(8)(ii)
137.	C	1926.758(c)
138.	D	1926.651(a)
139.	A	1926.703(a)(2)
140.	C	1926.703(e)(1)
141.	C	1926.1408, Table A
142.	C	1926.252 (b)
143.	B	1926.300(b)(4)(iv)(a)
144.	D	1926.450(b), See "Self-contained Adjustable Scaffold"
145.	C	1926.451(g)(1)
146.	B	1926.756(a)(1)

Q	Answer	Section #
147.	B	1926.451(c)(1) Note: Not more than 4:1 4 x 4 feet = 16 feet
148.	B	1926.552(b)(3), 1926.552(c)(7)
149.	D	1926.454, Subpart L Appendix A, Scaffold Specifications, General Guidelines and Tables, 1.(b)(i) – Table 1926.454, Subpart L Appendix A, Scaffold Specifications, General Guidelines and Tables, 1.(c) – Table
150.	C	1926.454, Subpart L Appendix A, Scaffold Specifications, 2. General Guidelines and Tables (s)(1)
151.	D	1926.302(a)(1)
152.	A	See "Kickout" in Glossary
153.	A	1926.454, Subpart L Appendix A, 1.(b)(ii)
154.	C	1926.502(d)(9)
155.	D	1926.454, Subpart L Appendix A, 1.(f)
156.	C	1926.404(b)(1)(ii)
157.	A	1926.604(2)(ii)
158.	A	1926.20(b)(3)
159.	A	1926.16(a) – (d)
160.	A	1926.50(d)(2), 1926.51(a)(4), 1926.51(c)(1), 1926.52, Table D-2
161.	D	1926.651(g)(1)(i)
162.	A	1926.250(b)(1), 1926.250(b)(6), 1926.250(b)(7), 1926.250(b)(8)(iv)
163.	D	1926.301(b) – (d)
164.	B	1926.302(e)(2)
165.	B	1926.1101(b), See "Asbestos-containing material" (ACM)
166.	B	1926.300(b)(2)
167.	D	1926.652(e)(2) or 1926.652(g)(2)
168.	B	1926.21(b)(1)
169.	D	1926.51(c)(4)
170.	C	1926.652, Subpart P Appendix A, (b), See "Moist Soil"
171.	D	1926.251(b)(6)(i)(D)
172.	C	1926.702(b)
173.	D	1926.150, Table F-1 – Fire Extinguishers Data
174.	D	1926.761, Subpart R Appendix D, (2)(i)

Q	Answer	Section #
175.	A	1926.302(e)(2)
176.	C	1926.152(d)(1)
177.	B	1926.454, Subpart L Appendix A, 2.(k)
178.	C	1926.502(b)(3)
179.	C	1926.451(h)(2)(ii)
180.	B	1926.302(b)(3)
181.	A	1926.302(a)
182.	C	1926.451(g)
183.	B	1926.452(w)(6)(i)
184.	B	1926.852(b)
185.	B	1926.452(h)(2)
186.	D	1926.502(f)(1)(i)
187.	C	1926.503, Subpart M Appendix A, (1)

NFPA 70 National Electrical Code, 2017
Practice Exam 1
Questions and Answers

1. Solar photovoltaic system dc circuits on or in one- and two-family dwellings shall be permitted to have a MAXIMUM voltage of _____ or less.

A. 125 volts
B. 250 volts
C. 300 volts
D. 600 volts

2. What is the MINIMUM height allowed for a fence enclosing an outdoor installation of 2,400-volt electrical equipment?

A. 6 feet
B. 7 feet
C. 8 feet
D. 9 feet

3. Where power for equipment is directly associated with the radio   frequency distribution system is carried by the coaxial cable, and the   power source is a power limiting transformer, what is the MAXIMUM   voltage this coaxial cable may carry?

A. 50 volts
B. 60 volts
C. 120 volts
D. 150 volts

4. Where a 15-ampere rated general-use ac snap switch is used as a disconnecting means for an ac motor of 2 HP or less, the NEC® requires the MAXIMUM full-load current rating of the motor to be NO more than _____.

A. 7.5 amperes
B. 10 amperes
C. 12 amperes
D. 15 amperes

5. Determine the MAXIMUM number of 125-volt, general-purpose receptacles the NEC® permits to be protected by a 20-ampere, 120-volt, single-pole inverse time circuit breaker in a commercial occupancy.

A. 18
B. 15
C. 13
D. 10

6. Which of the following statements, if any, is/are true regarding illumination for service equipment installed in electrical equipment rooms?

   I. The illumination shall not be controlled by means of three
      way switches.
   II. The illumination shall not be controlled by automatic means
      only.

A. I only
B. II only
C. both I and II
D. neither I nor II

7. In regard to the tenant spaces in a retail shopping mall; each occupant shall have access to the main disconnecting means, EXCEPT:

A. where the service and maintenance are provided by the building management and are under continuous building management supervision
B. where there are more than six disconnecting means provided.
C. where the primary feeder transformer does not exceed 600 volts.
D. where the secondary of the service transformer does not exceed
      240-volts to ground.

8. Determine the conductor allowable ampacity given the following conditions:

   * ambient temperature of 44 deg. C
   * 250 kcmil THWN copper conductors
   * four (4) current-carrying conductors are in the raceway
   * length of raceway is 25 feet

A. 160 amperes
B. 167 amperes
C. 200 amperes
D. 209 amperes

9. Determine the MAXIMUM overcurrent protection permitted for size 14 THWN copper motor control circuit conductors tapped from the load side of a motor overcurrent protection device. Given: the conductors require short-circuit protection and do not extend beyond the motor control equipment enclosure.

A. 20 amperes
B. 25 amperes
C. 30 amperes
D. 100 amperes

10. Circuit breakers rated _____ or less and 1000 volts or less shall have the ampere rating molded, stamped, etched or similarly marked into their handles or escutcheon areas.

A. 600 amperes
B. 200 amperes
C. 400 amperes
D. 100 amperes

11. In the kitchen of a dwelling unit where a single-phase, 125-volt, 15-or 20-ampere rated receptacle outlet is installed for a refrigerator and is located within 6 feet from the top inside edge of the bowl of the kitchen sink, the receptacle outlet shall be provided with _____.

A. GFCI protection only
B. AFCI protection only
C. both GFCI and AFCI protection
D. neither GFCI nor AFCI protection

12. Where a rooftop mounted air-conditioning unit is supplied with three (3) size 8 AWG THWN copper conductors, enclosed in an electrical metallic tubing (EMT) within three (3) inches of the rooftop, and exposed to direct sunlight and an ambient temperature of 100 degrees F, the allowable ampacity of the conductors is _____ .

A. 50 amperes
B. 44 amperes
C. 29 amperes
D. 25 amperes

13. Which of the following listed conductor insulations is oil resistant?

A. TW
B. TFE
C. THWN
D. MTW

14. All exposed non-current-carrying metal parts of an information technology system shall _____ or shall be double insulated.

A. be bonded to the equipment grounding conductor
B. not be bonded to the equipment grounding conductor
C. be bonded to the grounded conductor
D. be isolated

15. Determine the MINIMUM number of 15-ampere, 120-volt general lighting branch circuits required for 12,000 square feet multifamily condo where each dwelling unit has cooking facilities provided.

A. 15
B. 20
C. 24
D. 30

16. Storage batteries used as a source of power for emergency systems shall be of a suitable rating and capacity to supply and maintain the total load for at LEAST _____.

A. 1/2 hour
B. 1 hour
C. 1½ hours
D. 2 hours

17. When a conduit containing service-entrance conductors runs beneath a building, what is the MINIMUM depth of concrete required to cover the conduit for it to be considered "outside" the building?

A. 2 inches
B. 6 inches
C. 12 inches
D. 18 inches

18. The entire area of an aircraft hangar, including any adjacent and communicating areas not suitably cut off from the hangar, shall be classified as a Class I, Division 2 or Zone 2 location up to a level _____ above the floor.

A. 12 inches
B. 18 inches
C. 24 inches
D. 30 inches

19. Where a 240-volt, single-phase 90 ampere load is located 225 feet from a panelboard and supplied with size 3 THWN copper conductors; what does the approximate voltage drop on this circuit? (K = 12.9)

A. 6 volts
B. 4 volts
C. 8 volts
D. 10 volts

20. The continuity of the equipment grounding conductor system for portable electrical carnival equipment shall be verified _____.

A. and recorded on an annual basis
B. and recorded on a quarterly basis
C. and recorded on a monthly basis
D. each time the equipment is connected

21. Electrical services and feeders for recreational vehicle parks shall be calculated based on NOT less than _____ per RV site equipped with both 20-ampere and 30-ampere supply facilities.

A. 2400 volt-amperes
B. 9600 volt-amperes
C. 4800 volt-amperes
D. 3600 volt-amperes

22. In a commercial garage work area, which of the following 125-volt, single-phase receptacles, if any, are required to have GFCI protection?

I. 15-ampere general-purpose receptacles for hand tools and portable lighting equipment.
II. 20-ampere receptacles serving electrical diagnostic equipment only.

A. I only
B. II only
C. both I and II
D. neither I nor II

23. When sizing time-delay Class CC fuses for motor branch-circuit, short-circuit and ground-fault protection, they are to be sized at the same value as _____.

A. inverse-time circuit breakers
B. nontime-delay fuses
C. instantaneous trip circuit breakers
D. adjustable trip circuit breakers

24. The MINIMUM spacing required between the bottom of a 600 volt rated switchboard and the noninsulated busbars mounted in the switchboard cabinet is _____.

A. 6 inches
B. 8 inches
C. 10 inches
D. 12 inches

25. Given: A rigid metal conduit (RMC) to be installed will contain only
the following three (3) circuits on the load side of the service overcurrent protective devices:

 * two - 150 ampere, 3-phase circuits
 * one - 300 ampere, single-phase circuit

The load side equipment bonding jumper for this conduit must be a MINIMUM size of _____ copper.

A. 1 AWG
B. 2 AWG
C. 4 AWG
D. 6 AWG

Please See Answer Key on following page

1 Exam Prep
NFPA 70 National Electrical Code
Practice Exam 1
Questions and Answers

ANSWER KEY

Answer	Section/Page#
1. D	690.7
2. B	110.31
3. B	820.15
4. C	430.109(C)(2)

15 amperes x 80% = 12 amperes

5. C	220.14(I)

120 volts x 20 amps = 2,400 VA (circuit)
2,400 VA (circuit) ÷ 180 VA (one receptacle) = 13 outlets

6. B	110.26(D)
7. A	240.24(B)(1)
8. B	310.15(B)(2)
	Table 310.15(B)(16)
	Table 310.15(B)(2)(a)
	Table 310.15(B)(3)(a)

Size 250 kcmil THWN copper ampacity before derating = 255 amperes
255 amps x .82 (temp. correction) x .8 (adjustment factor) = 167.28 amperes

9. D	Table 430.72(B)
10. D	240.83(B)
11. C	210.8(A)(7)
	210.12(A)

Answer	Section/Page#
12. B	310.15(B)(2) Table 310.15(B)(2)(a) Table 310.15(B)(16)

outdoor ambient temperature = 100 deg. F
Note - A temperature correction factor of .88 must be applied.

Size 8 AWG THWN ampacity (before derating) = 50 amperes
50 amperes x .88 (temp. correction) = 44 amperes

13. D	Table 310.104(A)
14. A	645.15
15. B	Table 220.12 and 220.14(J)

12,000 sq. ft. x 3 VA = 36,000 VA (building)
120 volts x 15 amps = 1,800 VA (1 circuit)

$$\frac{36,000 \text{ VA (building)}}{1,800 \text{ VA (1 circuit)}} = 20 \text{ circuits}$$

16. C	700.12(A)
17. A	230.6(1)
18. B	513.3(B)
19. D	Chapter 9, Table 8 Voltage-drop formula

$$VD = \frac{2KID}{CM} \quad VD = \frac{2 \times 12.9 \times 90 \text{ amps} \times 225 \text{ ft.}}{52,620 \text{ CM}} = 9.92 \text{ volts dropped}$$

20. D	525.32
21. D	551.73
22. C	511.12
23. B	Table 430.52, Note 1
24. C	Table 408.5
25. C	250.102(D) 250.122(C) Table 250.122

1. Where conduits enter a floor-standing switchboard, switchgear or, panelboard at the bottom, the conduits, including their end fittings, shall NOT rise more than _____ above the bottom of the enclosure.

A. 6 inches
B. 4 inches
C. 2 inches
D. 3 inches

2. For emergency systems where internal combustion engines are used as the prime mover, an on-site fuel supply shall be provided with an on-site fuel supply sufficient for NOT less than _____ full-demand operation of the system.

A. 2 hours
B. 3 hours
C. 4 hours
D. 6 hours

3. Conductors supplying outlets for arc and xenon motion picture projectors of the professional type shall be a MINIMUM size of _____.

A. 12 AWG
B. 10 AWG
C. 8 AWG
D. 6 AWG

4. Thermostatically controlled switching devices serving as both controllers and disconnecting means for fixed electric space heating equipment shall _____.

A. be prohibited
B. be located not more than 5 feet above the floor level
C. directly open all grounded conductors when manually placed in the *OFF* position
D. be designed so that the circuit cannot be energized automatically after the device has been manually placed in the *OFF* position

5. A bonding jumper connected between the communications grounding electrode and power grounding electrode system at the building or structure service where separate electrodes are used shall NOT be smaller than size _____ copper.

A. 8 AWG
B. 6 AWG
C. 12 AWG
D. 10 AWG

6. Given: A straight pull of size 4 AWG and larger conductors is to made in a junction box that will have a trade size 3 in. conduit and two (2) trade size 2 in. conduits entering on the same side and exiting on the opposite wall. No splices or terminations will be made in the box. Which of the following listed junction boxes is the MINIMUM required for this installation?

A. 18 in. x 12 in.
B. 20 in. x 18 in.
C. 20 in. x 12 in.
D. 24 in. x 24 in.

7. Given: A dairy farm with a 120/240-volt, single phase electrical system will have the following three loads supplied from a common service; one – 18,000 VA, one - 16,000 VA, and one – 10,000 VA. What is the demand load, in amperes, on the ungrounded service-entrance conductors?

A. 183 amperes
B. 152 amperes
C. 304 amperes
D. 114 amperes

8. All 15- or 20-ampere, single-phase, 125-volt receptacles located within at LEAST _____ of the edge of a decorative fountain shall be provided with GFCI protection for personnel.

A. 10 feet
B. 15 feet
C. 20 feet
D. 25 feet

9. The emergency electrical disconnects for attended self-service gasoline stations or convenience stores with motor fuel dispensing facilities must be located NOT more than _____ from the motor fuel dispensers that they serve.

A. 20 feet
B. 50 feet
C. 75 feet
D. 100 feet

10. Given: A dry-type transformer is fed with four (4) parallel size 500 kcmil conductors per phase. The conductors enter the enclosure on the opposite wall of the terminals. What is the MINIMUM wire-bending space required for the conductors at each terminal?

A. 16 inches
B. 14 inches
C. 12 inches
D. 10 inches

11. What MINIMUM size THWN copper conductors are required to supply a continuous-duty, 25 hp, 208-volt, 3-phase motor, where the motor is on the end of a short conduit run that contains only three (3) conductors, at an ambient temperature of 115 deg. F?

A. 6 AWG
B. 3 AWG
C. 2 AWG
D. 1 AWG

12. Where time-delay (dual-element) fuses are used for short-circuit and ground-fault protection for both windings of a part-winding start induction motor, the fuses shall be permitted to have a rating NOT exceeding _____ of the full-load current of the motor.

A. 200 percent
B. 150 percent
C. 175 percent
D. 225 percent

13. Where a conductor is marked *RHW-2* on the insulation, what does the *-2* represent?

A. The cable has 2 conductors.
B. The conductor is double insulated.
C. The conductor has a nylon outer jacket.
D. The conductor has a maximum operating temperature of 90°C.

14. Apply the general method of calculation for dwellings and determine the demand load, in kW, on the ungrounded service-entrance conductors for four (4) household electric ranges rated 19 kW each.

A. 34 kW
B. 17 kW
C. 38 kW
D. 23 kW

15. In movie theaters, all switches for controlling the emergency lighting systems shall be located _____.

A. on the stage
B. in the lobby
C. in the manager's office
D. in the projection booth

16. Single-conductor cable Type _____ shall be permitted in exposed outdoor locations in photovoltaic source circuits for photovoltaic module interconnections within the photovoltaic array.

A. UF
B. THHN
C. USE-2
D. THWN

17. What percent of electrical supplied spaces in a recreational vehicle park must be equipped with at least one (1) 30-ampere 125-volt receptacle outlet?

A. 60 percent
B. 70 percent
C. 90 percent
D. 100 percent

18. Each operating room of a health care facility shall be provided with a MINIMUM of _____ listed "hospital grade" receptacles.

A. 12
B. 24
C. 30
D. 36

19. Where a 3-phase, 25 kVA rated transformer with a 480-volt primary and a 208Y/120-volt secondary is to be installed where both primary and secondary protection is required to be provided, determine the MAXIMUM standard ampere rating of the secondary overcurrent protection as permitted by the NEC®.

A. 80 amperes
B. 90 amperes
C. 100 amperes
D. 110 amperes

20. Where ungrounded conductors are run in parallel in multiple raceways, the equipment grounding conductor, where used, shall be _____.

A. omitted
B. run in parallel in each raceway
C. installed in one raceway only
D. bare

21. Where track lighting is installed in a continuous row, each individual section of NOT more than _____ in length shall have one additional support.

A. 2 feet
B. 4 feet
C. 6 feet
D. 8 feet

22. Determine the MINIMUM size THWN copper feeder conductors required by the NEC® to supply the following 480-volt, continuous duty, 3-phase, induction-type, Design C, motors.

* one - 40 hp
* one - 50 hp
* one - 60 hp

A. 2/0 AWG
B. 3/0 AWG
C. 4/0 AWG
D. 250 kcmil

23. In health care facilities, essential electrical systems shall have a MINIMUM _____.

A. of one (1) hour back-up time
B. capacity of 200 gallons of fuel for the auxiliary generator
C. of two (2) independent sources of power
D. capacity of 150 kVA

24. Where compressed natural gas vehicles are repaired in a commercial major repair garage, the area within _____ of the ceiling shall be considered unclassified where adequate ventilation is provided.

A. 18 inches
B. 24 inches
C. 30 inches
D. 36 inches

25. Where a 3-phase, 480-volt, 100 ampere demand load is located 390 feet from a panelboard, what MINIMUM size THWN aluminum conductors are required to supply the load where the voltage drop is required to be limited to 3 percent? (K = 21.2)

A. 2 AWG
B. 1 AWG
C. 1/0 AWG
D. 2/0 AWG

Please See Answer Key on following page

113

ANSWER KEY

Answer	Section/Page#
1. D	408.5
2. A	700.12(B)(2)
3. C	540.13
4. D	424.20(A)(3)
5. B	800.100(D)
6. D	314.28(A)(1)

3 in. (largest conduit) x 8 = 24 inches

7. B
        220.103
        Table 220.103
        Single-phase current formula

  18,000 VA x 100% = 18,000 VA
  16,000 VA x 75% = 12,000 VA
  10,000 VA x 65% =   6,500 VA
        Demand   =   36,500 VA ÷ 240 volts = 152 amperes

8. C	680.58
9. D	514.11(B)
10. A	312.6(B)(2)
	Table 312.6(B)

Answer	**Section/Page#**

11. D   Table 430.250
                            430.22
                            Table 310.15(B)(2)(a)
                            Table 310.15(B)(16)

25 hp motor FLC = 74.8 amperes x 125% = 93.5 amperes
93.5 amps /.75 (temperature correction) = 124.6 amperes
*NOTE: The wire size needs to be increased because of the elevated ambient
temperature. Size 1 AWG THWN conductors with an allowable ampacity of 130 amperes should be
selected.

12. B   430.4, Exception

13. D   Table 310.104(A)

14. D   Table 220.55 & Note 1

19 kW – 12 kW = 7 kW x 5% = 35% increase in Column C
17 kW (4 appliances in Col. C) x 135% = 22.95 kW demand

15. B   700.21 / 520.8

16. C   690.31(C)(1)

17. B   551.71(B)

18. D   517.19(C)(1)

19. B   3-Phase Current Formula
                            Table 450.3(B) Note 1
                            Table 240.6(A)

$$I = \frac{kVA \times 1000}{208 \times 1.732} \qquad I = \frac{25 \times 1,000}{208 \times 1.732} = \frac{25,000}{360.25} = 69.3 \text{ amperes}$$

69.3 amperes x 125% = 86.62 amperes

*NOTE: You are permitted to go up to the next standard size OCP device which has a rating of 90
amperes.

20. B   250.122(F)(b)

21. B   410.154

Answer	**Section/Page#**

22. C

Table 430.250
430.24(1) & (2)
Table 310.15(B)(16)

40 hp FLC = 52 amps x 100% = 52 amperes
50 hp FLC = 65 amps x 100% = 65 amperes
60 hp FLC = 77 amps x 125% = <u>96 amperes</u>
Total = 213 amperes

Size 4/0 AWG THWN conductors with an ampacity of 230 amperes should be selected.

23. C

517.41(A)

24. A

511.3(D)
Table 511.3(C)

25. C

Chapter 9, Table 8
3-phase voltage drop formula

*NOTE: 3% of 480 volts = .03 x 480 = 14.4 (voltage drop permitted)

$$CM = \frac{1.732 \times K \times I \times D}{VD \ permitted}$$

$$CM = \frac{1.732 \times 21.2 \times 100 \ amps \times 390 \ ft.}{14.4 \ volts} = 99,446 \ CM$$

Size 1/0 AWG conductors with a CMA of 105,600 should be selected.

NFPA 70 National Electrical Code, 2017
Practice Exam 3

1. A listed _____ shall be installed in or on all emergency systems switchboards and panelboards.

A. ground-fault circuit interrupter (GFCI)
B. surge-protective device (SPD)
C. arc-fault circuit interrupter (AFCI)
D. leakage-current detector-interrupter (LCDI)

2. In general, where a cablebus system is rated 95 amperes, the MAXIMUM allowable rating of the overcurrent device that may be used to protect the cablebus is _____.

A. 80 amperes
B. 90 amperes
C. 95 amperes
D. 100 amperes

3. A feeder tap less than 25 feet in length is not required to have overcurrent protection if the ampacity of the tap conductors is NOT less than _____ of the rating of the overcurrent device protecting the feeder conductors.

A. one-half
B. one-fourth
C. one-third
D. 75 percent

4. Given: A flexible metal conduit (FMC) to be installed will contain three (3) size 400 kcmil THWN copper conductors and one (1) size 250 kcmil copper conductor. Where the FMC is more than 24 inches long, what MINIMUM trade size FMC is permitted for this installation?

A. 3 in.
B. 3½ in.
C. 2½ in.
D. 4 in.

5. In general, which of the following MUST be provided at a patient bed location used for general care (Category 2) spaces in a hospital?

A. One branch circuit from the normal system.
B. One branch circuit from the critical branch of the essential electrical
   system.
C. "Hospital-grade" receptacles.
D. All of these.

6. When an electrical service is required to have a grounded conductor present, what is the smallest grounded conductor permitted for an electric service using size 1000 kcmil copper ungrounded conductors installed in a single raceway?

A. 3/0 copper
B. 2/0 copper
C. 1/0 copper
D. 4/0 copper

7. Determine the MINIMUM number of 20-ampere, 277-volt, general-lighting branch circuits required for a 150,000 square foot retail department store where the actual connected load is 400 kVA; consider circuit breakers of this size are NOT rated for continuous use.

A. 72
B. 82
C. 91
D. 102

8. Where a 2-gang box contains two (2) single-pole switches, unless the box is equipped with permanently installed barriers, voltage between the switches shall NOT be in excess of _____.

A. 120 volts
B. 300 volts
C. 480 volts
D. 240 volts

9. Where electrical metallic tubing (EMT) is installed under metal-corrugated sheet roofing decking, a clearance of at LEAST _____ must be maintained between the top of the tubing and the surface of the roof decking.

A. 1 in.
B. 1¼ in.
C. 1½ in.
D. 1¾ in.

10. Fluorescent luminaires installed MORE than _____ above the floor in patient care areas in a hospital, shall NOT be required to be grounded by an insulated equipment grounding conductor.

A. 6 feet
B. 6½ feet
C. 7 feet
D. 7½ feet

11. Where nonmetallic conduit is used to enclose conductors supplying a wet-niche luminaire located in a permanently installed swimming pool, a size _____ insulated copper grounding conductor shall be installed in the conduit, unless a listed low-voltage lighting system not requiring grounding is used.

A. 12 AWG
B. 10 AWG
C. 8 AWG
D. 6 AWG

12. The ampacity of phase conductors from the generator terminals to the first overcurrent device shall NOT be less than _____ of the nameplate current rating of the generator where the design of the generator does not prevent overloading.

A. 100 percent
B. 115 percent
C. 125 percent
D. 150 percent

13. In Class II, Division 1 locations, an approved method of connection of conduit to boxes or cabinets is _____.

A. compression fittings
B. threaded bosses
C. welding
D. all of these

14. The upward discharging vent of an underground fuel tank of motor fuel dispensing facilities is classified as a Class I, Division 1 location WITHIN _____ of the open vent, extending in all directions.

A. 3 feet
B. 5 feet
C. 6 feet
D. 8 feet

15. Conductors between the controller and the diesel engine of a fire pump are required to be _____.

A. 90 deg. C rated
B. 104 deg. C rated
C. stranded
D. solid

16. The allowable ampacity of a size 750 kcmil XHHW aluminum conductor when there are six (6) current-carrying conductors all of the same size and insulation in the raceway, installed in a dry location where the ambient temperature will reach 22 deg. C is _____.

A. 323.40 amperes
B. 365.40 amperes
C. 361.92 amperes
D. 348.00 amperes

17. Where multiple driven ground rods are used to form the grounding electrode system, in order to maintain an effective grounding electrode system, they shall NOT be less than _____ apart.

A. 4 feet
B. 6 feet
C. 8 feet
D. 10 feet

18. According to the NEC®, flat conductor cable (FCC) is permitted to be used for:

I. general-purpose circuit conductors.
II. appliance circuit conductors.

A. I only
B. II only
C. both I and II
D. neither I nor II

19. Determine the MINIMUM size USE aluminum cable permitted for use on an underground 120/240-volt, single-phase, service for a small office building that has a total load of 23,600 VA after all demand factors have been taken into consideration. Consider all conductor terminations are rated for 75 deg. C.

A. 1/0 AWG
B. 2/0 AWG
C. 1 AWG
D. 2 AWG

20. The MAXIMUM horizontal length of feeder tap conductors in a high-bay manufacturing building over 35 feet high at walls shall be _____.

A. 25 feet
B. 50 feet
C. 75 feet
D. 100 feet

21. Where an apartment complex has a connected lighting load of 205.4 kVA, what is the demand load, in kVA, on the ungrounded service-entrance conductors? Apply the portion of lighting load to which demand factor applies.

A. 60.2 kVA
B. 16.5 kVA
C. 63.0 kVA
D. 65.3 kVA

22. All of the following copper conductors are to be installed in an electrical metallic tubing (EMT) ten (10) feet long:

   * 24 - size 10 AWG THHW
   * 10 - size 10 AWG THHN
   * 14 - size 12 AWG THHN

Determine the MINIMUM trade size EMT required.

A. 2 in.
B. 2½ in.
C. 3 in.
D. 3½ in.

23. Given: A 40-unit apartment complex with a 120/240-volt, single-phase electrical system is to add a 6,000-watt, 240-volt, single-phase clothes dryer in each unit. How many amperes will the clothes dryers add to the ungrounded (line) service-entrance conductors when applying the general method of calculation?

A. 265 amperes
B. 270 amperes
C. 300 amperes
D. 350 amperes

24. When sizing fuses for a branch circuit serving a hermetic refrigerant motor-compressor, the device shall NOT exceed _____ of the rated load current marked on the nameplate of the equipment where the protection specified is not sufficient for the starting current of the motor.

A. 115 percent
B. 125 percent
C. 175 percent
D. 225 percent

25. Given: You are to install 90 feet of multioutlet assembly in the computer lab of a school where the computers are likely to be used simultaneously. Determine the MINIMUM number of 20-ampere, 120-volt, single-phase branch circuits required to supply the multioutlet assembly.

A. six
B. seven
C. eight
D. nine

Please See Answer Key on following page

1 Exam Prep
NFPA 70 National Electrical Code, 2017
Practice Exam 3
Questions and Answers

ANSWER KEY

Answer	Section/Page#
1. B	700.8
2. D	370.23
	240.4(B)(1), (2), & (3)
	Table 240.6(A)
3. C	240.21(B)&(B)(4)(3)
4. A	Chapter 9, Table 5
	Chapter 9, Table 4

250 kcmil THWN – 0.3970 sq. in. x 1 = 0.3970 sq. in.
400 kcmil THWN – 0.5863 sq. in. x 3 = <u>1.7589 sq. in.</u>
Total = 2.1559 sq. in.

A trade size 3 in. FMC with a permitted fill area of 2.827 sq. in.
@ 40% fill should be selected.

5. D	517.18(A)&(B)
6. B	250.24(C)(1)
	Table 250.102(C)(1)
7. C	210.19(A)(1)(a)
	210.11(A)

400 kVA x 1,000 = 400,000 VA
400,000 VA x 125% (continuous load) = 500,000 VA (bldg.)

277 volts x 20 amperes = 5,540 VA (one circuit)

<u>500,000 VA (bldg. lighting)</u> = 90.2 = 91 lighting circuits
   5,540 VA (one circuit)

*NOTE: Circuits need only to be installed to serve the connected load.

8. B	404.8(B)
9. C	300.4(E)

Answer	Section/Page#
10. D	517.13(B), Exception 3
11. C	680.23(B)(2)(b)
12. B	445.13
13. B	502.10(A)(1)
14. B	Table 514.3(B)(1)
15. C	695.14(D)
16. C	Table 310.15(B)(16) Table 310.15(B)(2)(a) Table 310.15(B)(3)(a)

Size 750 kcmil AL ampacity (before derating) = 435 amperes
435 amps x 1.04 (temp. correction) x .8 (adjustment factor) = 361.92 amperes

17. B	250.53(A)(3)
18. C	324.10(A)
19. C	Single-Phase Current Formula Table 310.15(B)(16)

$I = P \div E$ $I = 23,600$ VA $\div 240$ volts $= 98.33$ amperes

Size 1 AWG AL USE cable with an ampacity of 100 amperes should be selected.

20. A	240.21(B)(4)(2)
21. D	Table 220.42

Total lighting equals 205,400 VA
1st. 3000 VA @ 100 %   = 3,000 VA
next 117,000 VA @ 35%   = 40,950 VA
remainder [205.4 kVA - 120 kVA] = 85,400 VA @ 25%   = 21,350 VA
                                              Total demand = 65,300 VA

Answer	Section/Page#
22. A	Chapter 9, Table 5
	Chapter 9, Table 4

Size 10 AWG THHW = .0243 sq. in. x 24 = 0.5832 sq. in.
Size 10 AWG THHN = .0211 sq. in. x 10 = 0.2110 sq. in.
Size 12 AWG THHN = .0133 sq. in. x 14 = 0.1865 sq. in.
                                    Total = 0.9807 sq. in.

2 in. EMT with a 40% allowable fill of 1.342 sq. in. should be selected.

23. A	Table 220.54
	Single-phase current formula

Demand = 35% minus .5% for each dryer exceeding 23
40 dryers – 23 = 17 (exceeding 23) x .5% = 8.5%
35% - 8.5% = 26.5% demand

40 dryers x 6 kW = 240 kW x 26.5% (demand) = 63.6 kW
63.6 kW x 1000 = 63,600 watts

I = P ÷ E   I = 63,600 watts ÷ 240 volts = 265 amperes

24. D	440.22(A)
25. D	220.14(H)(2)
	645.5(A)
	210.19(A)(1)(a)

90 ft. x 180 VA per ft. x 125% = 20,250 VA (multioutlet assembly)

20 amps x 120 volts = 2,400 VA (one circuit)

$$\frac{20,250 \text{ VA (total load)}}{2,400 \text{ VA (one circuit)}} = 8.43 = 9 \text{ circuits}$$

NFPA 70 National Electrical Code, 2017
Practice Exam 4

1. Overcurrent protection for size 18 AWG non-power-limited fire alarm (NPLFA) circuit conductors shall NOT exceed _____ and the overcurrent protection for size 16 AWG NPLFA circuit conductors shall NOT exceed _____.

A. 8 amperes, 10 amperes
B. 7 amperes, 12 amperes
C. 8 amperes, 12 amperes
D. 7 amperes, 10 amperes

2. The general rule is where raceways and cables are exposed to direct sunlight on or above rooftops, and the distance above the roof to the bottom of the raceway or cable is less than 7/8 in., a temperature adder of 33°C (60°F) shall be added to the outdoor temperature to determine the applicable ambient temperature for application of the correction factors. An exception to this rule is _____.

A. prohibited
B. where the raceway or cables contain 3 or less current-carrying conductors
C. where the insulated conductors or cables have a temperature rating of
   90°C or more
D. where the insulated conductors or cables are Type XHHW-2

3. An emergency system is required to have NO more than, _____ to have power available in the event of failure of the normal supply system.

A. 10 seconds
B. 15 seconds
C. 60 seconds
D. 3 minutes

4. X-ray equipment installed in a hospital may be served by a hard-service cord with a suitable attachment plug, provided the branch circuit rating does NOT exceed _____.

A. 15 amperes
B. 20 amperes
C. 30 amperes
D. 50 amperes

5. Elevator driving motors used with a generator field control are rated as _____ duty motors.

A. intermittent
B. continuous
C. variable
D. controlled

6. Where a direct burial cable has a voltage of 45 kV, the NEC® mandates the MINIMUM burial depth of the cable to be at LEAST _____.

A. 24 inches
B. 36 inches
C. 42 inches
D. 48 inches

7. Given: A recreational vehicle campground has a total of 150 campsites with electrical power. Twenty-five (25) of the campsites are reserved as tent sites. How many sites are required to have at LEAST one (1) 20 ampere, 125-volt receptacle outlet?

A. 105
B. 125
C. 150
D. None

8. Determine the MINIMUM size type SO cord permitted as listed to supply a 40 hp, 460-volt, 3-phase, continuous-duty, ac wound rotor, motor installed in an area with an ambient temperature of 86 degrees F.

A. 2 AWG
B. 4 AWG
C. 6 AWG
D. 8 AWG

9. Where a 30 hp, 240-volt, 3-phase synchronous motor has a power factor of 90 percent, as per the NEC® the full-load running current of the motor is _____.

A. 63.0 amperes
B. 69.3 amperes
C. 76.23 amperes
D. 86.62 amperes

10. When water reaches the height of the established electrical datum plane for an irrigation pond, the electrical service equipment must _____.

A. be installed in a NEMA 6 enclosure
B. float
C. be installed in a NEMA 6P enclosure
D. disconnect

11. Disregarding exceptions, when installing emergency battery pack lighting unit equipment, the branch-circuit feeding this equipment shall:

A. be connected to the nearest receptacle outlet.
B. come from the closest outlet of power that is compatible with the
   emergency lights rated voltage.
C. be fed only from an identified emergency lighting panel.
D. be on the same branch-circuit serving the normal lighting in the area and connected ahead of any local switches

12. In an industrial establishment, what is the MAXIMUM length of 200 ampere rated busway that may be tapped to a 600-ampere rated busway without providing additional overcurrent protection?

A. 10 feet
B. 25 feet
C. 50 feet
D. 75 feet

13. Size 4/0 AWG, 75 deg. C aluminum secondary conductors of a 3-phase delta-wye transformer, shall be protected at NOT more than _____.

A. 175 amperes
B. 200 amperes
C. the calculated load connected to the transformer
D. none of these, because secondary protection is not required
   for multiphase, delta-wye transformer secondary conductors

14. For trade size 3/4 in. MI cable, the radius of the inner edge of the bend shall NOT be less than _____ times the external diameter of the cable.

A. three
B. four
C. five
D. seven

15. Where a flat cable assembly, Type FC, is installed LESS than _____ above the floor or fixed working platform, it shall be protected by a cover identified for the use.

A. 6 feet
B. 7 feet
C. 8 feet
D. 10 feet

16. The MINIMUM burial depth for conduit or cables installed under an airport runway, concourse or tarmac is _____.

A. 1½ feet
B. 2 feet
C. 3 feet
D. 4 feet

17. Determine the maximum initial size (no modifications necessary) overload protection required for a 480 volt, 3-phase, 15 hp, continuous-duty motor given the following related information:

 * Design C
 * temperature rise - 40 deg. C
 * service factor - 1.12
 * actual nameplate rating - 18 amperes

A. 20.7 amperes
B. 18.0 amperes
C. 22.5 amperes
D. 23.4 amperes

18. Assume where the overload protection you have selected on the above motor is not enough to start the motor and trips, therefore, modification of this value is necessary, determine the absolute MAXIMUM size overload protection permitted.

A. 22.5 amperes
B. 20.7 amperes
C. 25.2 amperes
D. 23.4 amperes

19. Where a 50-kVA transformer with a 480-volt, 3 phase primary and a 208Y/120-volt, 3-phase secondary is to be installed and overcurrent protection is required on both the primary and secondary side of the transformer; determine the MAXIMUM size overcurrent protection device permitted for the primary side.

A. 125 amperes
B. 150 amperes
C. 175 amperes
D. 200 amperes

20. What is the demand load, in VA, for the general-use receptacles in an office building that has a total of 150 general-use, 125-volt, 20-ampere, single-phase receptacle outlets installed?

A. 18,500 VA
B. 10,000 VA
C. 27,000 VA
D. 13,500 VA

21. Determine the MAXIMUM number of size 12 AWG conductors permitted to be housed in a 3½ in. deep, 3-gang masonry box that contains three (3) switches.

A. 21
B. 23
C. 24
D. 27

22. A horizontal raceway entering a dust-ignition proof enclosure from one that is not, need not have a seal-off if it is at LEAST_____ in length.

A. 18 inches
B. 5 feet
C. 10 feet
D. 25 inches

23. Where abandoned communications cables are identified for future use with a tag, the tag shall be _____.

A. red in color
B. orange in color
C. located outside the junction box
D. of enough durability to withstand the environment

24. All 125-volt, 15- and 20-ampere receptacles located within _____ of the inside walls of a storable pool, storable spa, or storable hot tub shall be protected by a ground-fault circuit interrupter.

A. 6 feet
B. 8 feet
C. 10 feet
D. 20 feet

25. A dry type transformer of 1000 volts or less and NOT exceeding _____ is permitted to be installed in a hollow space of a building, such as above a lift-out ceiling, provided there is adequate ventilation.

A. 25 kVA
B. 37½ kVA
C. 50 kVA
D. 112½ kVA

Please See Answer Key on following page

ALH 08/07/2019

1. D   760.43

2. D   310.15(B)(3)(c), Exception

3. A   700.12

4. C   517.71(A), Exception

5. A   620.61(B)(1)

6. C   Table 300.50, Column 1

7. C   551.71

8. A   430.6 & 6(A)(1)
                   Table 430.250
                   430.22
                   Table 400.5(A)(1), Column A

FLC of motor = 52 amperes x 125% = 65 amperes
Size 2 AWG SO cord with an ampacity of 80 amperes should be selected.

Note: T400.5(A)(1) #3 AWG to have ampacity of 70A

9. B   Table 430.250

63 amperes x 1.1 (power factor) = 69.3 amperes

10. D   682.11

11. D   700.12(F)(2)(3)

12. C   368.17(B), Exception

13. B   Table 310.15(B)(16)
                    240.4(B)(3)
                    Table 240.6(A)

Size 4/0 AWG AL conductors rated @ 75 deg. C ampacity = 180 amperes
Next standard size OCP is rated at 200 amperes.
*NOTE: Sec. 240.4(F) requires secondary OCP on delta-wye transformers.

14. C   332.24(1)

15. C   322.10(3)

16. A   Table 300.5, Column 1

17. C   430.6(A)(2)
                            430.32(A)(1)

     FLA of motor = 18 amps x 125% = 22.5 amperes

18. C   430.32(C)

     FLA of motor = 18 amps x 140% = 25.2 amperes

19. B   450.3(B)
                            Table 450.3(B)
                            Table 240.6(A)

$$I = \frac{kVA \times 1{,}000}{E \times 1.732} = \frac{50 \times 1{,}000}{480 \times 1.732} = \frac{50{,}000 \text{ VA}}{831.36} = 60.2 \text{ amperes}$$

     60.2 amperes x 250% = 150.5 amperes

20. A   220.14(I)
                            220.44
                            Table 220.44

150 receptacles x 180 VA = 27,000 VA
1st. 10,000 VA @ 100%   = 10,000 VA
(remainder) 17,000 VA @ 50%   = 8,500 VA
              TOTAL DEMAND = 18,500 VA

21. A   314.16(B)(4)
                            Table 314.16(A)

[masonry box] 9 (Size 12 AWG conductors permitted per gang)
            - 2 conductors per gang (switch)
        7 wires per box x 3 gang = 21 conductors

22. C   502.15(2)

23. D   800.25

24. D   680.32

25. C   450.13(B)

1. In Class II, Division 1 locations, where pendant mounted luminaires are suspended by rigid metal conduit (RMC) or intermediate metal conduit (IMC) and a means for flexibility is not provided, the conduit stems shall have a length of NOT more than _____.

A. 12 inches
B. 18 inches
C. 24 inches
D. 30 inches

2. All hydromassage bathtub metal piping systems and all grounded metal parts in contact with the circulating water associated with the bathtub shall be bonded together using a solid copper bonding jumper NOT smaller than _____.

A. 10 AWG
B. 8 AWG
C. 6 AWG
D. 12 AWG

3. Where power-limited fire alarm (PLFA) circuit conductors pass through a wall or floor, the conductors shall be protected by a metal raceway or nonmetallic conduit up to a height of at LEAST _____ above the floor, unless other means of protection is provided.

A. 8 feet
B. 6 feet
C. 7 feet
D. 10 feet

4. Luminaires installed in exposed or concealed locations under metal-corrugated sheet roof decking shall be installed and supported so there is NOT less than _____ clearance from the lowest surface of the roof decking to the top of the luminaire.

A. 1 in.
B. 1¼ in.
C. 1½ in.
D. 1¾ in.

5. Transformers with ventilation openings shall be installed so the ventilating openings are not blocked by walls or other obstructions. The required clearances shall be _____.

A. of not less than 3 inches
B. of not less than 6 inches
C. clearly marked on the transformer
D. as specified on the approved plans

6. Where a dwelling unit has a three (3) car attached garage, the NEC® requires a MINIMUM of _____ 125-volt, single-phase, 15- or 20-ampere receptacles to be installed in the garage.

A. one
B. two
C. three
D. four

7. With respect to messenger-supported service-drop conductors and open overhead wiring operating at 0 to 750 volts to ground, the MINIMUM vertical clearance that must be maintained from the base of a swimming pool diving
board and the conductors are _____.

A. 22½ feet
B. 19½ feet
C. 14½ feet
D. 10 feet

8. Determine the MINIMUM required size 75 deg. C rated conductors permitted to be used to supply a demand load of 200 amperes where provided with a 208Y/120-volt, 3-phase 4-wire, electrical system. Consider all four (4) conductors to be current-carrying and the ambient temperature is 120 deg. F.

A. 250 kcmil
B. 300 kcmil
C. 400 kcmil
D. 500 kcmil

9. A metal junction box to be installed will contain the following conductors:

* three - size 6 AWG ungrounded conductors
* three - size 6 AWG grounded conductors
* one size 8 AWG grounding conductor
* three - size 12 AWG ungrounded conductors
* three - size 12 AWG grounded conductors
* one - size 12 AWG grounding conductor

The junction box is required to have a volume of at LEAST _____.

A. 51.50 cubic inches
B. 53.75 cubic inches
C. 46.50 cubic inches
D. 56.50 cubic inches

10. In regard to permanently installed swimming pools, where necessary to employ flexible connections to a pool pump motor, _____ shall be permitted as the wiring method(s).

   I. UF cable
   II. liquidtight flexible metal conduit (LFMC)

A. I only
B. II only
C. neither I nor II
D. both I and II

11. Which of the following listed wiring methods is NOT approved for use in assembly locations, UNLESS encased in concrete?

A. EMT
B. Schedule 80 PVC
C. Type MC cable
D. Type AC cable

12. In regard to commercial garages, lamps and lampholders for fixed lighting located over lanes through which vehicles are commonly driven, shall be located NOT less than _____ above the floor level, unless the luminaires are of the totally enclosed type.

A. 8 feet
B. 10 feet
C. 12 feet
D. 14½ feet

13. Determine the maximum permitted operational setting of an adjustable inverse time circuit breaker used for branch-circuit, short-circuit and ground-fault protection of a 10 hp, 208-volt, 3-phase, squirrel cage, Design B, continuous-duty motor. Assume the motor will start at this setting and exceptions are not applicable.

A. 30.8 amperes
B. 35.7 amperes
C. 77.0 amperes
D. 338.8 amperes

14. Where transformer vaults are not protected with an automatic fire-suppression system, they shall be constructed of approved materials that have a MINIMUM fire-resistance rating of _____.

A. 1 hour
B. 2 hours
C. 3 hours
D. 4 hours

15. At a truck plaza, every electrified truck parking space intended to provide an electrical supply for transport refrigerated units, shall be equipped with a _____ receptacle outlet.

   I. 30 ampere, 480-volt, 3-phase, 3-pole, 4-wire
   II. 60 ampere, 208-volt, 3-phase, 3-pole, 4-wire

A. I only
B. II only
C. either I or II
D. both I and II

16. What is the MAXIMUM distance allowed to support intermediate metal conduit (IMC) from a junction box, where structural members do not readily permit fastening?

A. 3 feet
B. 5 feet
C. 6 feet
D. 8 feet

17. Explosionproof apparatus is required for electrical equipment placed in _____ locations.

A. Class I, Division 1 and 2
B. Class I Division 3
C. Class II, Division 1 and 2
D. all of these

18. Photovoltaic equipment shall be provided with isolating devices or equipment disconnecting means in circuits connected to equipment at a location within the equipment, or within sight and within _____ of the equipment.

A. 50 feet
B. 25 feet
C. 20 feet
D. 10 feet

19. Determine the MAXIMUM standard size inverse time circuit breaker permitted for branch-circuit, short-circuit, and ground-fault protection for a 50 hp, ac motor, when given the following related information.

* continuous-duty
* induction type
* 3-phase, 480 volt
* Design L
* nameplate rating 62 amperes

A. 175 amperes
B. 200 amperes
C. 250 amperes
D. 300 amperes

20. In general, on the load side of the point of grounding of a separately derived system such as a transformer, a grounded conductor is NOT permitted to be connected to _____.

A. equipment grounding conductors
B. normally noncurrent-carrying metal parts of equipment
C. ground, the earth
D. any of these

21. The life safety branch of the essential electrical system of a health care facility shall provide power to _____.

I. automatic doors used for building egress
II. illumination of electrical equipment rooms

A. I only
B. II only
C. both I and II
D. neither I nor II

22. Intrinsically safe apparatus, associated apparatus, and other equipment shall be installed
_____.

A. in accordance with the control drawings
B. in the electrical equipment room
C. on a backboard of at least 3/4 in. thick plywood
D. in a dedicated enclosure

23. The grounded conductor of a 3-phase, 3-wire, delta service shall have an ampacity NOT less
than _____.

A. that of the grounding conductor
B. that of the ungrounded conductors
C. 80 percent of the ungrounded conductors
D. 125 percent of the grounding conductor

24. Where a 150-kVA service transformer has a 480Y/277-volt, 3-phase primary and a
208Y/120-volt, 3-phase secondary, the full-load ampere rating on the primary side of the
transformer is _____.

A. 180 amperes
B. 312 amperes
C. 542 amperes
D. 416 amperes

25. Direct-buried cables or conductors located in a trench below 2-inch-thick concrete or
equivalent shall have a MINIMUM cover requirement of _____.

A. 6 inches
B. 12 inches
C. 18 inches
D. 24 inches

Please See Answer Key on following page
ALH 08/07/2019

1 Exam Prep
NFPA 70 National Electrical Code, 2017
Practice Exam 5
Questions and Answers

ANSWER KEY

Answer	Section/Page#
1. A	502.130(A)(3)
2. B	680.74(B)
3. C	760.130(B)(2)
4. C	410.10(F)
5. C	450.9
6. C	210.52(G)(1)
7. A	Table 680.9(A)
8. C	Table 310.15(B)(16)
	Table 310.15(B)(2)(a)
	Table 310.15(B)(3)(a)

$$\frac{200 \text{ amperes (load)}}{.75 \text{ (temp. cor.)} \times .8 \text{ (adj. factor)}} = \frac{200}{.6} = 333 \text{ amperes}$$

Size 400 kcmil conductors with an ampacity of 335 amperes should be selected from Table 310.15(B)(16).

9. C	314.16(B)(1) & (5)
	Table 314.16(B)

6 AWG ungrounded conductors	- 3 x 5.00 cu. in.	= 15.00 cu. in.
6 AWG grounded conductors	- 3 x 5.00 cu. in.	= 15.00 cu. in.
8 AWG grounding conductor	- 1 x 3.00 cu. in.	= 3.00 cu. in.
12 AWG ungrounded conductors	- 3 x 2.25 cu. in.	= 6.75 cu. in.
12 AWG grounded conductors	- 3 x 2.25 cu. in.	= 6.75 cu. in.
12 AWG grounding conductor	- 1 x -0- cu. in.	= -0- cu. in.
	TOTAL	= 46.50 cu. in.

10. B	680.21(A)(2)
11. B	518.4(A)

Answer	**Section/Page#**
12. C	511.7(B)(1)(b)
13. C	430.6(A)(1) Table 430.250 Table 430.52

FLC of 10 hp motor = 30.8 amperes x 250% = 77 amperes

14. C	450.42
15. C	626.31(C)
16. B	342.30(A)(2)
17. A	500.7(A)
18. D	690.15(A)
19. C	430.6(A)(1) Table 430.250 430.52(C)(1), Exception 2(c) Table 240.6(A)

FLC of 50 hp motor = 65 amperes x 400% = 260 amperes

20. D	250.30(A)
21. A	517.33 517.33(H)
22. A	504.10(A)
23. B	250.24(C)(3)
24. A	3-phase Current Formula

$$I = \frac{kVA \times 1{,}000}{E \times 1.732} = \frac{150 \times 1{,}000}{480 \times 1.732} = \frac{150{,}000}{831.36} = 180.32 \text{ amperes}$$

25. C	Table 300.5, Column 1

NFPA 70 National Electrical Code, 2017
Practice Exam 6

1. The lightning protection system ground terminals shall be bonded to the building or structure grounding electrode system. The bonding shall be _____ and to all raceways, boxes, and enclosures between the cabinets or equipment and the grounding electrode.

A. insulated from one end
B. insulated at each end
C. bonded at both ends
D. bonded at one end only

2. Type AC cable shall provide an adequate path for:

A. grounding conductors.
B. fault current.
C. water drainage.
D. a grounding electrode.

3. A totally enclosed ac motor located in a Class I, Division 1 location shall _____.

A. be double insulated
B. be located no more than 5 ft. above the floor
C. have a temperature rise of not more than 40°C
D. be supplied with positive air ventilation

4. Color coding shall be permitted to identify intrinsically safe conductors where they are colored _____ and where no other conductors of the same color are used.

A. orange
B. light blue
C. yellow
D. green

5. Mandatory rules of the NEC® are those that identify actions that are specifically required or prohibited, are characterized by the use of the terms _____.

A. shall or shall not
B. may or may not
C. will or will not
D. can or cannot

6. A surge arrestor is required on each ungrounded conductor of an industrial facility that experiences severe thunderstorms. If the electrical system is a 4-wire, wye-connected grounded system, how many surge arrestors shall be required?

A. one
B. two
C. three
D. four

7. As per the NEC®, a _____ location may be temporarily subject to dampness and wetness.

A. dry
B. damp
C. moist
D. wet

8. High-impedance grounded neutral systems shall be permitted for 3-phase ac systems of 480-volts to 1,000 volts where _____.

A. the conditions of maintenance ensure that only qualified persons service the installation
B. ground detectors are installed on the electrical system
C. line-to-neutral loads are not served
D. all of these conditions are met

9. Where the overcurrent protection specified is not sufficient for the starting current of an air-conditioner motor-compressor, the rating or setting shall be permitted to be increased but shall not exceed _____ of the motor-rated-load current or branch circuit selection.

A. 225%
B. 175%
C. 125%
D. 115%

10. Floor duct installed in the concrete floor of an aircraft hangar shall be classified as a _____ location.

A. Class II, Division2
B. Class II, Division 1
C. Class I, Division 2
D. Class I, Division 1

11. Generally, where installed on the outside of a raceway, the length of the equipment bonding jumper shall NOT exceed _____ and shall be routed with the raceway.

A. 4 feet
B. 6 feet
C. 5 feet
D. 8 feet

12. Unless otherwise permitted by the local authority having jurisdiction, Type AC cable shall be secured within _____ of every box, cabinet, or fitting and at intervals not exceeding 4½ ft. where installed on or across framing members.

A. 8 inches
B. 18 inches
C. 12 inches
D. 24 inches

13. Energized electrical equipment operating at 120-volts to ground with exposed live parts on one side and a concrete block tile wall on the other side of the working space, is Condition _____.

A. one
B. two
C. three
D. four

14. Where corrosion protection is necessary and rigid metal conduit (RMC) or intermediate metal conduit (IMC) is threaded in the field, the threads shall be coated with a/an _____ material compound.

A. grounding
B. moisture-resistant
C. non-conductive, corrosion-resistant
D. approved, electrically conductive, and corrosion-resistant

15. In general, flexible metal conduit (FMC) shall be supported by an approved means at intervals NOT exceeding _____.

A. 1 foot
B. 3 feet
C. 4½ feet
D. 6 feet

16. The accessible portions of abandoned supply circuits and interconnecting cables for information technology equipment, or any systems in an information technology equipment room, shall be _____.

A. removed unless contained in a metal raceway
B. required to be secured in place
C. protected by a nonmetal covering
D. tagged to avoid potential damage

17. Disregarding exceptions, the maximum distance permitted for seven (7) current-carrying Type NM cables to be bundled together without requiring the allowable ampacity of the conductors to be reduced is _____.

A. 12 inches
B. 24 inches
C. 30 inches
D. 36 inches

18. For other than dwelling units, all single-phase, 125-volt, 15- and 20-ampere receptacle outlets shall be calculated at NOT less than _____ for each single or for each multiple receptacle mounted on one yoke.

A. 100 VA
B. 150 VA
C. 180 VA
D. 200 VA

19. Where underground installed service conductors emerge from grade and are exposed to physical damage, which of the following listed raceways are NOT approved for such use?

A. rigid metal conduit
B. Schedule 80 PVC
C. Schedule 40 PVC
D. RTRC-XW

20. One who has skills and knowledge related to the construction and operation of the electrical equipment and installations and has received safety training to recognize and avoid the hazards involved, is defined in the NEC® as a/an _____ person.

A. exposed
B. knowledgeable
C. safety certified
D. qualified

21. Cable splices made and insulated by approved methods are permitted to be located within a cable tray, provided they are _____.

A. accessible
B. copper conductors only
C. conductors with a temperature rating of not less than 90°C
D. exposed to ambient temperatures of not more than 110°F

22. Transformers containing oil or a liquid that will burn where located in Class I, Division 1 locations shall be _____.

A. enclosed in a fence
B. installed in vaults only
C. identified for Class I locations
D. installed in a fire-proof room

23. Given: A 240-volt, single-phase, 5,000 VA non-motor operated appliance is supplied by a circuit with size 8 AWG Type NM cable. The MAXIMUM standard rating permitted for a circuit breaker providing overcurrent protection for this appliance is _____.

A. 30 amperes
B. 35 amperes
C. 40 amperes
D. 45 amperes

24. What is the general lighting demand load, in VA, on the ungrounded (line) service entrance conductors of an industrial commercial (loft) building having dimensions of 100 ft. by 300 ft.?

A. 60,000 VA
B. 75,000 VA
C. 90,000 VA
D. 105,000 VA

25. According to the NEC®, when an installation uses metal conduits entering service equipment or enclosures with concentric or eccentric knockouts, as a MINIMUM requirement, the raceway(s) shall be equipped with _____.

A. double locknuts
B. single locknuts
C. at least one locknut and one bushing
D. bonding jumpers, and bonding-type locknuts or bushings

Please See Answer Key on following page
ALH 08/12/2019

1 Exam Prep
NFPA 70 National Electrical Code, 2017
Practice Exam 6
Questions and Answers

ANSWER KEY

Answer	Section/Page#
1. C	250.64(E)(1) 250.106
2. B	320.108
3. D	501.125(A)(2)
4. B	504.80(C)
5. A	90.5(A)
6. C	280.3
7. A	Article 100 – Definitions
8. D	250.36(1)-(3)
9. A	440.22(A)
10. D	513.8(A)
11. B	250.102(E)(2)
12. C	320.30(B)
13. B	Table 110.26(A)(1)
14. D	300.6(A)
15. C	348.30(A)
16. A	645.5(G)
17. B	310.15(B)(3)(A)
18. C	220.14(I)
19. C	300.5(D)(4)
20. D	Article 100 – Definitions

21. A   392.56

22. B   501.100(A)(1)

23. C   Table 310.15(B)(16)
                                         334.80

The overcurrent protection is to be not less than the ampacity of the conductors.

24. B   Table 220.12
                                         Article 100 – Definitions
                              230.42(A)(1)

100 ft. x 300 ft. = 30,000 sq. ft. x 2 VA = 60,000 VA
60,000 VA x 125% (continuous load) = 75,000 VA demand load

25. D   250.92(B)(1)-(4)

1. As a general rule, for an ac electrical system operating at less than 1000 volts, a main bonding jumper shall connect the grounded conductor(s) to _____.

A. each service disconnecting means grounded conductor terminal
B. each meter base only
C. the grounding electrode
D. each sub-panel

2. Every circuit breaker having an interrupting rating other than _____ shall have its interrupting rating shown on the circuit breaker.

A. 20,000 amperes
B. 15,000 amperes
C. 10,000 amperes
D. 5,000 amperes

3. Electrically operated residential kitchen waste disposers shall be permitted to be cord-and-plug connected however, the flexible cord is to be not less than 18 inches in length and NOT over _____ in length.

A. 36 inches
B. 48 inches
C. 30 inches
D. 24 inches

4. Excluding neon signs, branch circuits that supply all other electric signs and outline lighting systems shall be rated NOT to exceed _____.

A. 40 amperes
B. 30 amperes
C. 20 amperes
D. 25 amperes

5. When considering the support distance for rigid metal conduit (RMC), in compliance with the rules established by the NEC®, what is the MAXIMUM
horizontal unsupported length permitted of a trade size 2 in. raceway?

A. 16 feet
B. 10 feet
C. 12 feet
D. 14 feet

6. Generally, receptacle outlets provided for the small appliance countertop or work surface circuits in the kitchen of a dwelling shall be located above the countertop or work surface, but NOT more than_____ above the countertop or work surface.

A. 6 inches
B. 12 inches
C. 18 inches
D. 20 inches

7. What is the general lighting demand load, in VA, on the ungrounded (line) service entrance conductors, of a building consisting of four (4) offices each having a floor space of 20 feet by 30 feet?

A. 8,400 VA
B. 7,200 VA
C. 4,800 VA
D. 10,500 VA

8. For electrical systems of 1,000 volts or less, overhead spans of open individual conductors up to 50 feet in length and not supported by a messenger wire, shall be at LEAST size _____ copper.

A. 8 AWG
B. 10 AWG
C. 6 AWG
D. 12 AWG

9. An unbroken length of rigid metal conduit (RMC) or intermediate metal conduit (IMC) is permitted to support a luminaire in a billboard sign in lieu of a box where the _____.

A. luminaire is at least 8 feet above grade or standing area when
    accessible to unqualified persons
B. length of conduit exceeds 4 feet from the last point of conduit support
C. luminaire is 15 inches in any direction from a single conduit entry
D. total support weight on a single conduit exceed 20 pounds

10. Isolated ground receptacles that incorporate an isolating grounding conductor connection intended for the reduction of electrical noise or electromagnetic interference, shall be clearly identified by a/an _____ located on the front or face of the receptacle.

A. red circle
B. orange triangle
C. red triangle
D. yellow happy face

11. A mobile home that is factory-equipped with gas or oil-fired central heating equipment and cooking appliances may be provided with a listed mobile home power-supply cord NOT less than _____.

A. 50 amperes
B. 40 amperes
C. 60 amperes
D. 100 amperes

12. The sum of the cross-sectional areas of all contained conductors at any cross-section of a nonmetallic wireway shall NOT exceed _____ of the interior cross-sectional area of the wireway.

A. 40%
B. 30%
C. 60%
D. 20%

13. The disconnecting means for motors and their controllers shall open _____ conductors of the circuit.

A. the "A" phase
B. the grounded
C. the "B" phase
D. simultaneously all ungrounded phase

14. Where a feeder system includes a short run of trade size 1 in. listed liquidtight flexible metal conduit (LFMC), the circuit conductors contained in the LFMC must be protected by overcurrent devices rated NOT more than _____ in order for the LFMC to be an approved type of equipment grounding conductor.

A. 30 amperes
B. 20 amperes
C. 60 amperes
D. 80 amperes

15. A general-use, 125-volt, 15-ampere rated receptacle located in a hallway of a dwelling unit is required to be _____.

A. listed tamper-resistant
B. on a dedicated circuit
C. replaced with a 20-ampere rated receptacle
D. provided with GFCI protection

16. Type NM cable is permitted for use under all the following conditions or locations EXCEPT:

A. as a feeder.
B. in Type V construction.
C. in a wet or damp location.
D. in a multifamily dwelling unit.

17. According to the NEC®, which MINIMUM enclosure type letter would be required where the installation is a motor controller located outdoors, in an area that is subject to heavy rain and snow?

A. Type 1
B. Type 3
C. Type 4
D. Type 6

18. Given: A commercial building provided with a 208Y/120-volt, 3-phase, electrical system has a calculated demand load of 72,200 VA; the ungrounded (phase) service entrance conductors must have an ampacity of at LEAST _____.

A. 200 amperes
B. 350 amperes
C. 300 amperes
D. 250 amperes

19. As per the NEC®, the definition of a motor controller is _____.

A. a device to open the circuit automatically on a predetermined overcurrent
B. an interconnected combination of equipment that provides a means of adjusting the motor speed
C. a device which allows circuit conductors to be disconnected from their source of supply
D. a device to stop or start a motor by making or breaking the current

20. What is the MINIMUM of 20-ampere, 120-volt, general lighting branch circuits required for a dwelling unit having a lighting load of 9,600 VA?

A. three
B. five
C. four
D. two

21. Where a sub-panel is fed with CU Type NM cable and the circuit is protected by a 60 ampere overcurrent protective device, in compliance with the NEC®, the equipment grounding conductor should be at LEAST size _____.

A. 12 AWG
B. 10 AWG
C. 8 AWG
D. 6 AWG

22. A service disconnect may be installed in all of the following locations, EXCEPT _____.

A. outdoors
B. an exit foyer
C. a bathroom
D. a residential garage

23. Where a sign in a public parking lot is fed with 200 ampere, 120/240-volt, single phase, service conductors installed in a rigid metal conduit (RMC), what is the MINIMUM required burial depth of the conduit?

A. 24 inches
B. 12 inches
C. 18 inches
D. 30 inches

24. Where all of the multiconductor cables are smaller than 4/0 AWG, the sum of the cross-sectional areas of all cables shall NOT exceed _____ when installed in a 9 inch wide ladder-type cable tray.

A. 7.0 sq. in.
B. 10.5 sq. in.
C. 14.0 sq. in.
D. 21.0 sq. in.

25. Conduit bodies enclosing size 6 AWG or smaller conductors shall have a cross-sectional area NOT less than _____ than the cross-sectional area of the largest conduit or tubing to which they are attached.

A. 1.25 times larger
B. 1.50 times larger
C. 1.75 times larger
D. 2.00 times larger

Please See Answer Key on following page

Answer	Section#
1. A	250.24(C)
2. D	240.83(C)
3. A	422.16(B)(1)(2)
4. C	600.5(B)(2)
5. A	Table 344.30(B)(2)
6. D	210.52(C)(5)
7. D	Table 220.12 230.42(A)(1)

20 ft. x 30 ft. = 600 sq. ft. per office x 3.5 VA = 2,100 VA
2,100 VA x 4 offices = 8,400 VA x 125% (continuous load) = 10,500 VA demand

8. B	225.6(A)(1)
9. A	314.23(F), Ex. 2(1)-(6)
10. B	406.3(D)
11. B	550.10(A), Exception 1
12. D	378.22
13. D	430.103
14. C	250.118(6)(c)
15. A	406.12(1) 210.52
16. C	334.12(B)(4)
17. B	Table 110.28

18. A   3-phase current formula
                          I = VA ÷ E x 1.732

    I = $\frac{7,200 \text{ VA}}{208 \times 1.732}$ = $\frac{7,200}{360}$ = 200 amperes

19. D   430.2

20. C   Trade knowledge

    120 volts x 20 amperes = 2,400 VA (one circuit)

    $\frac{9,600 \text{ VA (load)}}{2,400 \text{ VA (ckt.)}}$ = 4 circuits

21. B   Table 250.122

22. C   230.70(A)(2)

23. A   Table 300.5, Column 2

24. B   392.22(A)(1)(b)
                               Table 392.22(A), Column 1

25. D   314.16(C)(1)

157

1. An acceptable color for conductors intended for use as ungrounded conductors is _____.

A. white
B. gray
C. green
D. orange

2. A metal underground water pipe is permitted for use as a grounding electrode where the water pipe is in direct contact with the earth for at LEAST _____ or more.

A. 3 feet
B. 6 feet
C. 8 feet
D. 10 feet

3. For low-voltage lighting systems operating at 30 volts or less, the output circuits of the power supply are to be rated for NOT more than _____.

A. 20 amperes
B. 25 amperes
C. 30 amperes
D. 15 amperes

4. Where a 12-kW portable generator is used for temporary wiring on a construction site, which of the following listed single-phase, 125-volt receptacle outlets are mandated to provide ground-fault circuit-interrupter protection for personnel?

A. All 20- and 30-ampere rated receptacles.
B. Only one 20-ampere rated receptacle.
C. Two 20-ampere rated receptacles.
D. Only one 30-ampere rated receptacle.

5. An unintentional, electrically conducting connection between an ungrounded conductor of an electrical circuit and the normally non-current-carrying conductors, metallic enclosures, metallic raceways, metallic equipment or earth is referred to as a _____ in the NEC®.

A. grounded conductor
B. short
C. ground-fault
D. bonding jumper

6. Where GFCI protection is not provided, ceiling-suspended (paddle) fans are NOT permitted to be located _____.

A. in a kitchen
B. in a garage
C. under an open porch
D. over a spa or hot tub, less than 12 ft. above the maximum water level

7. Which of the following underground installed buried metal pipes is approved for use as a grounding electrode?

I. A water pipe, in direct contact with the earth for 8 ft.
II. A gas pipe, in direct contact with the earth for 30 ft.

A. I only
B. II only
C. both I and II
D. neither I nor II

8. For an overhead type motor fuel dispensing device located at a service station or a convenience store, the space within the dispenser enclosure shall be classified as a _____ location.

A. Class I, Division 2
B. Class I, Division 1
C. Class 2, Division 2
D. Class 2, Division 1

9. Disregarding exceptions, and assume the modification of the value you select is not necessary, determine the MAXIMUM trip setting permitted for the overload devices used to protect a 3-phase, 10 hp, 208-volt, continuous-duty motor with a FLA of 28 amperes and a temperature rise of 46°C marked on the motor nameplate.

A. 30.8 amperes
B. 38.5 amperes
C. 35.0 amperes
D. 32.2 amperes

10. The neutral conductor is ALWAYS:

A. connected to the neutral point of an electrical system.
B. a grounding conductor.
C. a bonding conductor.
D. an ungrounded conductor.

11. The overcurrent protection for feeders and branch circuits that serve electric vehicle supply equipment, shall be sized at NOT less than _____ of the maximum load of the electric vehicle supply equipment.

A. 115%
B. 150%
C. 125%
D. 175%

12. Stationary ac motors require the _____ where installed in a Class I, Zone 2 atmosphere that is considered a hazardous or classified location.

A. motor disconnecting means shall be within 5 feet of the motor
B. frame of the motor shall be grounded
C. the wiring method to consist of rigid metal conduit (RMC)
D. motor disconnecting means to be unfused

13. Given: A rigid metal conduit (RMC) originates in an area that is unclassified, then passes through a Class I, Division 1 area, and finally terminates in a panelboard located in an unclassified area. The RMC is without any connections or fittings when passing through the Class I, Division 1 area or within a foot on either size of the boundary of the Class I, Division1 location. How many seal-off fittings are required in this conduit run?

A. none
B. one
C. two
D. three

14. Given: A 3-phase, 240-volt delta system is balanced with a 15 kVA load per phase (45,000 VA total load). What is the line current in amperes?

A. 249.3 amperes
B. 144.3 amperes
C. 120.4 amperes
D. 108.2 amperes

15. Where switches or circuit breakers are used as the main disconnecting means for a building service, they shall be installed such that the center of the grip of the operating handle of the switch or circuit breaker, when in its highest position, is NOT more than _____ above the floor or working platform.

A. 6 feet
B. 7 feet
C. 6 feet, 6 inches
D. 6 feet, 7 inches

16. The service equipment for a mobile home shall have an ampere rating of NOT less than _____ at 120/240-volts, single-phase.

A. 200 amperes
B. 60 amperes
C. 100 amperes
D. 150 amperes

17. Which of the following is NOT a requirement for an intersystem bonding termination?

A. It is provided with not less than three terminals.
B. It shall be connected to the meter enclosure only, with a minimum size 8 AWG conductor.
C. The terminals shall be listed for grounding and bonding.
D. The terminals shall be accessible for connection and inspection.

18. For 120-volt, 15- and 20-ampere branch circuits, the rating of any one (1) cord-and-plug connected utilization equipment not fastened in place shall NOT exceed _____ of the branch circuit ampere rating.

A. 80 percent
B. 70 percent
C. 60 percent
D. 50 percent

19. The National Electrical Code® requires ventilation of a battery room where batteries are being charged to prevent _____.

A. battery corrosion
B. electrostatic charge
C. deterioration of the building steel
D. an accumulation of an explosive mixture

20. Where a building has a service rated at 1,200 amperes and multiple driven ground rods are used as part of the grounding electrode system, what is the MINIMUM size copper conductor that may be used to bond the ground rods together?

A. 8 AWG
B. 6 AWG
C. 4 AWG
D. 2 AWG

21. All 15- and 20-ampere, 125 and 250-volt, nonlocking receptacles located in a wet location shall be listed _____ type.

A. weather proof
B. waterproof
C. weather-resistant
D. water-resistant

22. Where liquidtight flexible metal conduit (LFMC) is used to connect equipment where flexibility is necessary to minimize the transmission of vibration from equipment or to provide flexibility for equipment that requires movement after installation _____.

A. an equipment grounding conductor is not needed
B. an equipment grounding conductor should be installed outside the flexible
    metal conduit
C. the raceway must be used as the equipment grounding conductor.
D. an equipment grounding conductor shall be installed

23. Luminaires shall be installed so that adjacent combustible material is not subjected to temperatures in excess of _____.

A. 60°C
B. 75°C
C. 90°C
D. 110°C

24. A household gas furnace with a one (1) hp motor protected with a circuit breaker accessible to the user, does NOT require a disconnecting means if _____.

A. provided with a unit switch that disconnects all ungrounded conductors
B. provided with GFCI protection
C. the circuit breaker is rated for 20 amperes or less
D. located on the same floor level with the circuit breaker

25. In switchboards and panelboards, a 3-pole circuit breaker or fusible switch shall be considered _____.

A. as an independent circuit
B. as 3 overcurrent protection devices
C. a bi-directional breaker
D. a back-fed overcurrent device

*** Please See Answer Key on following page ***

Answer	Section#

1. D   200.6(A)&(B)
200.119
310.110(C)

2. D   250.52(A)(1)

3. B   411.3

4. A   590.6(A)(3)

5. C   Article 100 –Definitions

6. D   680.43(B)(1)(a)

7. D   250.52(A)(1)
250.52(B)(1)

8. B   Table 514.3(B)(1)

9. D   430.32(A)(1)

     Nameplate FLA rating – 28 amperes x 115% = 32.2 amperes

10. A   Article 100 – Definitions

11. C   625.40

12. B   430.242(3)

13. A   501.15(A)(4), Exception 1

14. D   3-phase current formula
$I = P \div E \times 1.732$

$$I = \frac{45{,}000 \text{ VA}}{240 \times 1.732} = \frac{45{,}000}{416} = 108.2 \text{ amperes}$$

15. D   240.24(A)
404.8(A)

16. C	550.32(C)
17. B	250.94(A)(1)-(6)
18. A	210.23(A)(1)
19. D	480.10(A)
20. B	250.66(A)
21. C	406.9(A)
22. D	250.118(6)(e)
23. C	410.11
24. A	422.34
25. B	408.54

1. When calculating the service entrance conductors for a farm service, the second largest load of the total load, shall be computed at _____.

A. 90 percent
B. 80 percent
C. 75 percent
D. 65 percent

2. When used in a non-power limited fire alarm circuit (NPLFA), what is the MAXIMUM size overcurrent protective device that may be used for a size 18 AWG conductor?

A. 7 amperes
B. 10 amperes
C. 15 amperes
D. 8 amperes

3. Installation of information technology equipment remote disconnecting controls shall NOT be required for critical operations data systems when several conditions are in place including _____.

A. an emergency fire detection system
B. an approved fire suppression system suitable for the application
C. an engineer has given approval
D. when the equipment is installed in a room with a 3 hour fire rating

4. What is the term used for electrical equipment or materials to which a symbol has been attached, or other identifying mark of an organization that is acceptable to the authority having jurisdiction?

A. labeled
B. listed
C. rated
D. approved

5. Rooms or areas of dwelling units shall be protected by a listed arc-fault circuit interrupter (AFCI), combination type, installed to provide protection of the _____.

A. service
B. panelboard
C. feeder circuit
D. entire branch circuit

6. All receptacles located within at LEAST _____ of a therapeutic tub shall be provided with GFCI protection.

A. 10 feet
B. 5 feet
C. 6 feet
D. 15 feet

7. When applying the general method of calculations for a dwelling unit having four (4) or more fastened in place appliances, other than electric ranges, dryers, space heating equipment, or air-conditioning equipment, it shall be permissible to apply a demand factor of _____ when sizing the service conductors.

A. 50 percent
B. 60 percent
C. 75 percent
D. 65 percent

8. Branch circuits that supply electric signs shall be considered _____ loads for the purposes of calculations.

A. continuous
B. non-continuous
C. full-current
D. intermittent

9. Additional services shall be permitted for a single building or other structure sufficiently large to make two (2) or more services necessary if permitted by _____.

A. the registered design professional
B. qualified personnel
C. the engineer of record
D. special permission

10. Which of the following statements are true for transformers serving electric discharge lighting having a rating of more than 1,000 volts?

A. The transformers are not required to be accessible.
B. The transformers should be installed as near to the lamps as practicable.
C. The secondary voltage shall be a maximum of 16,000 volts.
D. The maximum secondary current rating shall not exceed 120 mil amperes.

11. Assuming the use of THWN copper conductors and terminations rated for 75°C, determine the MINIMUM feeder conductor size when given the following related information:

• 120-volt, single-phase system
• one (1) 30 ampere continuous load
• one (1) 5 ampere non-continuous load

A. 4 AWG
B. 8 AWG
C. 6 AWG
D. 10 AWG

12. As a general rule, all conductors of a multiwire branch circuit shall originate from the same panelboard, simultaneously disconnect all ungrounded conductors and supply only line-to-_____ loads.

A. neutral
B. ground
C. line
D. hot

13. In general, for newly installed grounded systems, where branch circuits or feeders supply separate buildings or structures, equipment grounding conductors are _____.

A. required
B. not required
C. required only on 3-phase systems
D. not required if a ground rod is installed

14. Given: An underground run of PVC conduit with size 4 AWG conductors is the wiring method used to supply an air-conditioning unit that is protected by an overcurrent protective device rated 60 amperes. What is the MINIMUM size copper equipment grounding conductor that must be installed in the PVC?

A. 10 AWG
B. 12 AWG
C. 6 AWG
D. 8 AWG

15. The service disconnecting means for each electrical service shall consist of NOT more than _____ switches or circuit breakers.

A. one
B. two
C. three
D. six

16. Utilization equipment weighing not more than 6 pounds is permitted to be supported to any box or plaster ring secured to a box, provided the equipment or its supporting yoke is secured with at LEAST two (2) _____ or larger screws.

A. No. 10
B. No. 8
C. No. 6
D. No. 12

17. Photovoltaic systems operating at _____ dc or greater between any two conductors shall be protected by a listed PV arc-fault circuit interrupter or other system components listed to provide equivalent protection.

A. 24 volts
B. 50 volts
C. 80 volts
D. 120 volts

18. In general, for household electric ranges with a rating of 8¾ kW or more, the MINIMUM branch-circuit rating shall be _____.

A. 30 amperes
B. 40 amperes
C. 50 amperes
D. 45 amperes

19. Each doorway leading into a transformer vault from the building interior shall be provided with a tight-fitting door that has a minimum fire rating of three (3) hours. However, if the transformer vault is protected with an automatic sprinkler system, the construction rating of _____ shall be permitted.

A. 2 hours
B. 2½ hours
C. 1 hour
D. 1½ hours

20. Where a 240-volt, single-phase, 5 kW storage-type water heater is located in the basement of a dwelling, and the load-center panelboard is located outdoors, a disconnect in the basement for the water heater is _____.

A. required
B. not required
C. not permitted
D. permitted but not required

21. What is the MAXIMUM ampere rating permitted for a 125-volt, single-phase, receptacle outlet having a cord-and-plug connected motor load that does not have individual overload protection?

A. 20 amperes
B. 30 amperes
C. 25 amperes
D. 15 amperes

22. After all demand factors have been taken into consideration and calculations completed, a one family dwelling with a 120/240-volt, single-phase electrical system has a demand load of 35,000 VA. The MINIMUM size THWN copper ungrounded (line) conductors required for an underground installed service lateral is _____.

A. 1 AWG
B. 1/0 AWG
C. 2/0 AWG
D. 3/0 AWG

23. Which of the following shall be permitted in the dedicated electrical space above a switchboard or panelboard?

A. air-conditioning ducts
B. sprinkler protection
C. leak protection
D. water piping

24. Which of the following 3-phase systems would be allowed to be a high-impedance grounded neutral system where a resistor limits the ground-fault current to a low value?

A. 230-volts
B. 208Y/120-volts
C. 480-volts
D. 480Y/277-volts

25. Boxes for use on electrical systems over 1000 volts, shall be closed by suitable covers securely fastened in place. An underground metal box cover that weighs over _____ shall be considered meeting this requirement.

A. 75 pounds
B. 80 pounds
C. 90 pounds
D. 100 pounds

Please See Answer Key on following page

<u>Answer</u>	<u>Section#</u>
1. C	Table 220.103
2. A	760.43
3. B	645.10(B)(4)
4. A	Article 100 – Definitions
5. D	210.12(A)(1)
6. C	680.62(E)
7. C	220.53
8. A	600.5(B)
9. D	230.2(B)(2)
10. B	410.144(B)
11. B	215.2(A)(1)(a) Table 310.15(B)(16)

30 amp continuous load x 125%   = 37.5 amperes
5 amp non-continuous load x 100% =   5.0 amperes
                 Total load   = 42.5 amperes

Size 8 AWG THWN conductors with an ampacity of 50 amperes should be selected from Table 310.15(B)(16).

12. A	210.4(C)
13. A	250.32(B)(1)
14. A	250.122(A) Table 250.122
15. D	230.71(A)
16. C	314.27(D), Exception
17. C	690.11
18. B	210.19(A)(3)

19. C   450.43(A), Exception

20. A   422.31(B)

21. D   430.42(C)

22. A   Single-phase current formula $I = P \div E$
                                      310.15(B)(7)(1)
                                      Table 310.15(B)(16)

$$I = \frac{36{,}000 \text{ VA}}{240 \text{ volts}} = 145.8 \text{ amperes} \times .83 = 121 \text{ amperes}$$

Size 1 AWG THWN CU conductors with an ampacity of 130 amperes should be selected from Table 310.15(B)(16).

23. B   110.26(E)(1)(a)&(c)

24. C   250.36

25. D   314.72(E)

1. At carnivals and fairs, service equipment shall not be installed in a location that is accessible to unqualified persons, UNLESS the equipment _____.

A. has a voltage to ground of not more than 125 volts
B. is provided with GFCI protection
C. is lockable
D. is installed at a height of more than 6 feet

2. Where the NEC® specifies that one equipment shall be "within sight from" or "within sight of" another equipment, the specified equipment is to be visible and NOT more than _____ from the other.

A. 50 feet
B. 100 feet
C. 125 feet
D. 200 feet

3. As a general rule, where a cable is installed parallel to framing members, the cable shall be installed so that the nearest edge of the cable is NOT less than _____ from the nearest edge of the framing member.

A. ¾ in.
B. 1 in.
C. 1¼ in.
D. 1½ in.

4. Generally, how many grounded conductors are permitted to be terminated under an individual terminal within a switchboard or panelboard where the equipment operates at less than 1,000 volts?

A. four
B. three
C. two
D. one

5. The service equipment provided for a mobile home shall be located in sight from and NOT more than _____ from the exterior wall of the mobile home it serves.

A. 50 feet
B. 30 feet
C. 75 feet
D. 100 feet

6. In regard to power sources for Class 2 and Class 3 circuits, a dry cell battery shall be considered an inherently limited Class 2 power source, provided the voltage is _____ or less and the capacity is equal to or less than that available from series connected No. 6 carbon zinc cells.

A. 30 volts
B. 24 volts
C. 12 volts
D. 18 volts

7. Where electrical boxes are installed in a wall having a combustible finish and located above a kitchen wall countertop they shall be installed _____.

A. recessed ¼ in.
B. recessed a minimum of ½ in.
C. projected out not less than ¼ in. from the finish surface
D. flush or projected from the finish surface

8. A single-phase, 125-volt, 15- or 20-ampere receptacle outlet shall be installed at each residential kitchen, breakfast room, or dining room wall countertop and work surface that is at LEAST _____ or wider.

A. 12 inches
B. 24 inches
C. 36 inches
D. 20 inches

9. A one-family dwelling unit is to have the following fastened in place appliances installed:

      1,200 VA dishwasher
      4,000 VA water heater
      1,150 VA garbage disposer
      700 VA attic fan
      1,920 VA garage door opener

The demand load, in VA, on the ungrounded (line) service entrance conductors for the listed appliances is _____ when applying the general method of calculations for dwelling units.

A. 7,728 VA
B. 6,728 VA
C. 6,276 VA
D. 8,970 VA

10. Nonmetallic cable trays shall be made of _____ material.

A. fire-resistant
B. waterproof
C. fire-proof
D. flame-retardant

11. Switches are to be located a horizontal distance of at LEAST _____ from the inside walls of an indoor placed spa or hot tub.

A. 4 feet
B. 5 feet
C. 8 feet
D. 10 feet

12. Direct buried cables installed under an open field vacant property must have a MINIMUM cover depth of _____ when the applied voltage is not more than 600 volts.

A. 24 inches
B. 18 inches
C. 12 inches
D. 30 inches

13. Shore power for boats docked in marinas and boatyards shall be provided by single receptacles that are of the locking- and grounding-type, mounted at least 12 inches above the deck surface, and rated NOT less than _____.

A. 50 amperes
B. 40 amperes
C. 30 amperes
D. 20 amperes

14. For electrical systems over 1000 volts, where pulls of conductors in junction boxes are being made, the length of the box shall NOT be less than _____ the outside diameter of the largest shielded or lead-covered conductor or cable entering the box.

A. 8 times
B. 12 times
C. 32 times
D. 48 times

15. Each grounding electrode plate of bare or electrically conductive coated iron or steel material shall expose NOT less than _____ sq. ft. of surface to exterior soil.

A. 1
B. 1½
C. 2
D. 3

16. Installation of direct buried cables in an area that is subject to movement by frost or settlement of the soil shall be _____.

A. prohibited
B. of copper conductors only
C. placed with "S" loops or provide an adequate allowance for movement
D. placed on running boards of pressure-treated wood or of nonmetallic material

17. Busways shall be securely supported at intervals NOT exceeding _____ unless the raceway is otherwise designed and marked.

A. 6 feet
B. 8 feet
C. 4 feet
D. 5 feet

18. At LEAST _____ of free conductor, measured from the point in the box where it emerges from its raceway, shall be left at each junction box or device box for splices or connections to devices.

A. 4 inches
B. 6 inches
C. 8 inches
D. 12 inches

19. Where fixed wiring above bulk storage tanks is installed in PVC conduit, the PVC shall be _____.

A. Schedule 20
B. Schedule 40
C. Schedule 80
D. Schedule 100

20. Electrical installations which are controlled by lock(s) or other approved means, shall be considered to be accessible to _____.

A. personnel with a key
B. qualified persons only
C. personnel with authority
D. building inspectors and first responders

21. The size of an equipment grounding conductor of the wire type is based on the _____.

A. line voltage
B. conductor resistance
C. line inductance
D. the rating of the branch-circuit, short-circuit, and ground-fault protective
   device

22. The NEC® mandates expansion fittings for rigid PVC conduit shall be provided to compensate for thermal expansion. In an environment where the normal annual change in temperature is 100°F, and the length of the PVC is 100 feet, how much allowance for thermal expansion must be considered?

A. 4.06 inches
B. 6.08 inches
C. 3.04 inches
D. 8.11 inches

23. Where an enclosure housing a motor controller is located outdoors and subjected to exposure to heavy rain, sleet and snow, the enclosure must be listed as a _____ enclosure.

A. Type 1
B. Type 3
C. Type 4
D. Type 6

24. The MINIMUM clearance between luminaires installed in clothes closets and the nearest point of a closet storage space shall be _____ where surface-mounted incandescent or LED luminaires are installed.

A. 24 inches
B. 18 inches
C. 12 inches
D. 6 inches

25. For commercial buildings, industrial occupancies and multifamily dwellings, at least one (1) 125-volt, single-phase, 15- or 20-ampere rated receptacle outlet shall be installed NOT more than _____ from the indoor electrical service equipment.

A. 6 feet
B. 10 feet
C. 25 feet
D. 50 feet

Please See Answer Key on following page

1 Exam Prep
NFPA 70 National Electrical Code, 2017
Practice Exam 10 - Answers

Answer	Section#
1. C	525.10(A)
2. A	Article 100 - Definitions
3. C	300.4(D)
4. D	408.41
5. B	550.32(A)
6. A	725.121(A)(5)
7. D	314.20
8. A	210.52(C)(1)
9. B	220.53

```
 1,200 VA dishwasher
 4,000 VA water heater
 1,150 VA garbage disposer
   700 VA attic fan
 1,920 VA garage door opener
 8,970 VA connected load x 75% (demand factor) = 6,728 VA demand load
```

Answer	Section#
10. D	392.100(F)
11. B	680.43(C)
12. A	Table 300.5, Column 1
13. C	555.19(A)(4)
14. D	314.71(A)
15. C	250.52(A)(7)
16. C	300.5(J),(IN.)
17. D	368.30
18. B	300.14
19. C	515.7(A)

20.	B	110.31
21.	D	250.122(A)
		Table 250.122
22.	A	Table 352.44
23.	B	Table 110.28
24.	C	410.16(C)(1)
25.	C	210.64

1. PVC conduit shall be securely fastened within _____ of each outlet, junction device, conduit body, or other conduit termination box.

A. 3 feet
B. 4 feet
C. 5 feet
D. 6 feet

2. A hazardous location where easily ignitible fibers or materials producing combustible flyings are handled, manufactured, or used, but where they are not likely to be in suspension in the air in quantities sufficient to produce ignitible mixtures is recognized as a _____ location in the NEC®.

A. Class I
B. Class II
C. Class III
D. Class IV

3. A copper-clad steel rod type grounding electrode shall be at LEAST _____ in diameter.

A. 3/8 in.
B. 1/2 in.
C. 5/8 in.
D. 3/4 in.

4. Given: A single-phase, 120/240-volt service of a single-family dwelling has a chain-link metal fence opposite exposed live parts of the service equipment. The required depth of the working space in front of the service equipment must be at LEAST _____.

A. 2 ft. 6 in.
B. 3 ft.
C. 3 ft. 6 in.
D. 4 ft.

5. Tap conductors for a recessed luminaire shall be in a suitable raceway or Type AC or MC cable having a length NOT to exceed _____.

A. 4 feet
B. 6 feet
C. 5 feet
D. 8 feet

6. Where exposed Type NM cable passes through a floor, the cable shall be protected from physical damage by an approved means extending at LEAST _____ above the floor.

A. 10 inches
B. 8 inches
C. 12 inches
D. 6 inches

7. When used as a direct buried feeder cable, which of the following wiring methods is permitted for use to supply a water well pump located 50 feet from a dwelling?

A. Type NM cable
B. Type AC cable
C. Type TC cable
D. Type UF cable

8. The supply to a portable switchboard on a stage shall be by means of listed extra-hard usage cords or cables. Single-conductor portable supply cable sets used for this purpose shall NOT be smaller than _____.

A. 2 AWG
B. 4 AWG
C. 6 AWG
D. 8 AWG

9. The MINIMUM clearance for overhead feeder conductors, less than 1,000 volts, that pass above commercial areas subject to truck traffic is _____.

A. 10 feet
B. 12 feet
C. 15 feet
D. 18 feet

10. In regard to fixed electric space-heaters, factory-assembled nonheating leads of heating cables, if any, shall be at LEAST _____ in length.

A. 10 feet
B. 6 feet
C. 7 feet
D. 8 feet

11. Where the heating, air-conditioning or refrigeration equipment is installed on the roof of a commercial, industrial, or an apartment building, a single-phase, 125-volt, 15- or 20-ampere rated receptacle outlet ____.

A. is required to be located within 100 ft. from the equipment
B. may be connected to the line side of the equipment disconnecting means, provided the receptacle is equipped with GFCI protection
C. shall be located on the same level and within 25 ft. of the equipment
D. is permitted to be connected to the load side of the equipment disconnecting means, if within 10 ft. of the equipment and GFCI protected.

12. Given: An existing 150 kVA transformer with a 208Y/120-volt, 3-phase, secondary has a full-load current of 220 amperes per phase. What approximate additional single-phase load, per phase, may be added to the secondary side of the transformer?

A. 180 amperes
B. 196 amperes
C. 416 amperes
D. 334 amperes

13. The conductors in multiconductor portable cables, of over 600 volts nominal, used to connect mobile equipment and machinery, shall be at LEAST size _____ copper or larger and employ flexible stranding.

A. 14 AWG
B. 12 AWG
C. 10 AWG
D. 8 AWG

14. In metal raceways or enclosures, all conductors of feeders using a common neutral shall be enclosed within the same raceway or enclosure, with a MAXIMUM of _____ sets of 3-wire feeders permitted to utilize a common neutral.

A. two
B. three
C. four
D. five

15. Where a flat cable assembly, Type FC, is installed LESS than _____ above the floor level or fixed working platform, it shall be protected by a cover identified for the use.

A. 6 feet
B. 7 feet
C. 8 feet
D. 10 feet

16. On a 4-wire, 3-phase, wye circuit where more than _____ of the load consists of nonlinear loads such a fluorescent lighting, there are harmonic current present in the neutral conductor and the neutral conductor shall be considered to be a current-carrying conductor.

A. 50 percent
B. 30 percent
C. 25 percent
D. 10 percent

17. Where direct-buried conductors emerge from below grade and extend up a pole, the conductors must be protected by raceways up to a height of 8 feet above finished grade and in no case shall protection be required to exceed _____ below finished grade.

A. 18 inches
B. 12 inches
C. 24 inches
D. 36 inches

18. Given: After all demand factors have been taken into consideration, a small office building with a single-phase, 120/240-volt electrical system has a demand load of 35,000 watts. The MINIMUM size copper conductors with THW insulation required for the ungrounded (line) service entrance conductors is _____.

A. 3 AWG
B. 1/0 AWG
C. 2/0 AWG
D. 3/0 AWG

19. According to the NEC®, the ampacity of a conductor is the current, in amperes, that the conductor can carry continuously under the conditions of use without exceeding its _____.

A. voltage rating
B. power rating
C. temperature rating
D. insulation rating

185

20. Where a building or structure is supplied by more than one (1) service from the local utility company:

A. a fire pump shall be installed.
B. a permanent plaque shall be installed at each service disconnect location denoting all other services.
C. an optional standby system shall be installed.
D. all of the above shall be installed.

21. In Class I, Division 1 locations, all threaded conduit and fittings referred as National Standard Pipe Taper (NPT) thread that are entries into explosionproof equipment shall be made up with at LEAST _____ fully engaged threads.

A. five
B. three
C. four
D. six

22. Where the service entrance conductors for a commercial building or an industrial facility are size 350 kcmil aluminum with XHHW insulation, what MINIMUM size copper grounding electrode conductor is required?

A. 6 AWG
B. 4 AWG
C. 2 AWG
D. 1 AWG

23. Where a wall-mounted central vacuum system is cord-and-plug connected to a single-phase, 125-volt, 20-ampere receptacle located in an attached garage of a residence, the receptacle shall be provided with _____ protection.

A. only AFCI
B. only GFCI
C. both AFCI and GFCI
D. only LCDI

24. For track lighting in other than dwelling units, or guest rooms of hotels and motels, a load of _____ shall be calculated for every two (2) feet of lighting track or fraction thereof.

A. 200 VA
B. 180 VA
C. 150 VA
D. 120 VA

25. Where a galvanized rigid metal conduit (RMC) is used as a driven or buried grounding electrode, it shall be a MINIMUM trade size _____ and not less than 8 ft. in length.

A. ½ in.
B. 1 in.
C. 1¼ in.
D. ¾ in.

*****Please See Answer Key on following page*****

<u>Answer</u>	<u>Section#</u>
1. A	352.30(A)
2. C	500.5(D)
3. C	250.52(A)(5)(b)
4. B	Table 110.26(A)(1)
5. B	410.117(C)
6. D	334.15(B)
7. D	340.10(1) 334.12(B)(4) 320.12(2) 336.12(4)
8. A	520.54(C)
9. D	225.18(4)
10. C	424.34
11. C	210.63
12. B	3-phase current formula

$$I = \frac{power}{E \times 1.732} \qquad I = \frac{150 \times 1000}{208 \times 1.732} \qquad = \frac{150,000}{360} = 416 \text{ amperes FLC}$$

416 amperes (available FLC) – 220 amperes (existing load) = 196 amperes

13. B	400.31(A)
14. B	215.4(A)
15. C	322.10(3)
16. A	310.15(B)(5)(c)
17. A	300.5(D)(1)

18. B   Single-phase current formula
$$I = P \div E$$
Table 310.15(B)(16)

$$I = \frac{35,000 \text{ VA}}{240 \text{ volts}} = 145.8 \text{ amperes}$$

Size 1/0 THW CU conductors with an ampacity of 150 amperes should be selected from Table 310.15(B)(16).

19. C   Article 100 – Definitions

20. B   230.2(E)

21. A   500.8(E)(1)

22. C   250.66
Table 250.66

23. B   210.8(A)(2)

24. C   220.43(B)

25. D   250.52(A)(5)(a)

1. All of the following wiring methods are permitted to be present in a ceiling space used as a return-air plenum EXCEPT _____.

A. Type AC cable
B. PVC conduit
C. IMC conduit
D. Type MI cable

2. Cabinets housing overcurrent protective devices shall NOT be located _____.

A. over uneven surfaces
B. over stairway landings
C. over steps of a stairway
D. under a mezzanine

3. For the purpose of determining conductor fill in a device box, a three-way switch is counted as equal to _____ conductor(s), based on the largest conductor connected to the switch.

A. one
B. two
C. three
D. four

4. A transformer vault is required to be provided with a door sill or curb with a height of NOT less than _____.

A. 6 inches
B. 8 inches
C. 2 inches
D. 4 inches

5. Single-phase, 125-volt, 15- and 20-ampere receptacle outlets installed in floors of dwelling units shall not be counted as part of the required number of receptacle outlets, if they are located more than _____ from the wall.

A. 18 inches
B. 12 inches
C. 30 inches
D. 24 inches

6. Where practicable, overhead CATV coaxial cables attached to a building shall be separated from lightning conductors by at LEAST _____.

A. 2 feet
B. 4 feet
C. 6 feet
D. 5 feet

7. Grounding conductors and bonding jumpers shall NOT be connected by _____.

A. exothermic welding
B. pressure connectors
C. machine screw-type fasteners
D. sheet metal screws

8. Determine the MAXIMUM standard size time-delay fuses permitted for branch-circuit, short-circuit and ground-fault protection for a 50 hp, 3-phase, 460-volt, induction-type motor with a FLA rating of 61 amperes marked on the nameplate.

A. 100 amperes
B. 110 amperes
C. 115 amperes
D. 125 amperes

9. Each commercial occupancy accessible to pedestrians shall be provided with at least one sign outlet supplied by a branch circuit rated at LEAST _____.

A. 15 amperes
B. 20 amperes
C. 30 amperes
D. 40 amperes

10. The MAXIMUM number of size 14 AWG TW conductors permitted in a trade size 3/8 in. flexible metal conduit (FMC) without fittings inside the FMC is _____.

A. five
B. two
C. three
D. four

11. Class 1 power-limited conductors of MINIMUM size _____ shall be permitted to be used, provided they supply loads that do not exceed the ampacities give in 402.5 and are installed in a raceway, an approved enclosure, or a listed cable.

A. 18 AWG
B. 22 AWG
C. 28 AWG
D. 16 AWG

12. Luminaires mounted in the walls of a permanently installed swimming pool, shall be installed with the top of the luminaire lens NOT less than _____ below the normal water level of the pool, unless the luminaire is listed and identified for use at lesser depths.

A. 12 inches
B. 18 inches
C. 20 inches
D. 24 inches

13. A point on a wiring system at which current is taken to supply fixtures, receptacles, lamps, luminaires, heaters, motors and other utilization equipment is considered _____.

A. an outlet
B. a supply
C. a junction
D. a termination

14. A ground ring consisting of a size 2 AWG bare copper conductor encircling the building or structure is permitted for use as a grounding electrode however, the conductor must have a length of 20 feet or more and be buried below the earth's surface at a depth of NOT less than _____.

A. 24 inches
B. 18 inches
C. 36 inches
D. 30 inches

15. Apply the optional method of calculations for dwelling units and determine the demand load, in kW, on the ungrounded (line) service entrance conductors where an eight (8) unit multifamily condo has an 8 kW electric range in each unit.

A. 27.52 kW
B. 28.80 kW
C. 32.00 kW
D. 26.88 kW

16. In the patient bed location in the general care (Category 2) spaces of a health care facility, each patient bed location shall be supplied by at least two (2) branch circuits, and the branch circuits ___.

A. should be provided with AFCI protection
B. shall not be part of a multiwire branch circuit
C. must have isolated equipment grounded conductors
D. shall supply only single receptacle outlets

17. Which of the following statements regarding vertically-installed circuit breakers, if any, are TRUE?

I. The breakers shall be closed (ON) when in the up position.
II. The breakers shall clearly indicate when they are ON or OFF.

A. I only
B. II only
C. both I and II
D. neither I nor II

18. Extreme _____ may cause PVC conduit to become brittle, and therefore more susceptible to damage from physical contact.

A. sunlight
B. corrosive conditions
C. heat
D. cold

19. According to the NEC®, if used to connect to equipment where flexibility is necessary after installation, trade size ¾ in. flexible metal conduit (FMC) will require additional support if the FMC exceeds _____ from the last point where the FMC is securely fastened.

A. 5 feet
B. 4 feet
C. 3 feet
D. 2 feet

20. In an aircraft storage hangar, the area that extends upward from the floor to a level _____ above the surface of aircraft wings, power plants and fuel tanks shall be classified as a Class I, Division 2 or Zone 2 location.

A. 5 feet
B. 6 feet
C. 8 feet
D. 10 feet

21. For new installations in residential outdoor areas where permanently installed swimming pools are located, ceiling-suspended (paddle) fans installed above the pool or the area extending 5 feet horizontally from the inside walls of the pool, shall be installed at a height of NOT less than _____ above the maximum water level of the swimming pool.

A. 10 feet
B. 12 feet
C. 15 feet
D. 8 feet

22. For conductors of more than 1000 volts, multiconductor or multiplexed single-conductor cables having individual shielded conductors, the MINIMUM bending radius is _____ times the diameter of the individually shielded conductors or 7 times the overall diameter, whichever is greater.

A. 10
B. 15
C. 16
D. 12

23. Where equipment grounding conductors are installed in parallel in multiple metallic raceways, they shall be sized in accordance with _____ of the NEC®.

A. Table 250.66
B. Table 250.122
C. Table 310.15(B)(16)
D. Table 310.15 (B)(17)

24. Where chain-link metal fences are surrounding an electrical substation and located within a MINIMUM distance of _____ from the exposed electrical conductors or equipment, the fence shall be bonded to the grounding electrode system.

A. 20 feet
B. 25 feet
C. 16 feet
D. 22 feet

25. In the NEC®, an enclosure constructed so that moisture will not enter the enclosure under specified test conditions is referred to as _____.

A. weatherproof
B. watertight
C. water-repellant
D. water-resistant

Please See Answer Key on following page

1 Exam Prep
NFPA 70 National Electrical Code, 2017
Practice Exam 12 - Answers

Answer	Section#
1. B	300.22(C)(1)
2. C	240.24(F)
3. B	314.16(B)(4)
4. D	450.43(B)
5. A	210.52(A)(3)
6. C	820.44(E)(3)
7. D	250.8(A)
8. D	430.6(A)(1) Table 430.250 Table 430.52 430.52(C)(1), Exception 1 Table 240.6(A)

FLC of motor = 65 amperes x 175% = 113.75 amperes
The next standard size fuses with a rating of 125 amperes should be selected.

| 9. B | 600.5(A) |
| 10. D | Table 348.22 |

3 - #14 TW + 1 #14 TW equipment grounding conductor = 4 - #14 TW

11. A	725.49(A)
12. B	680.23(A)(5)
13. A	Article 100 – Definitions
14. D	250.53(F)
15. A	Table 220.84

8 kW x 8 units = 64 kW x 43% (demand factor) = 27.52 kW demand

| 16. B | 517.18(A) |

17. C   240.81

18. D   352.10, IN.

19. C   348.30(A), Exception #2(1)

20. A   513.3(C)(1)

21. B   680.22(B)(1)

22. D   300.34

23. B   250.122(A)&(F)

24. C   250.194(A)

25. B   Article 100 – Definitions

NFPA 70 National Electrical Code, 2017
Final Exam 1

1. Given: After all demand factors have been taken into consideration for an office building, the demand load is determined to be 90,000 VA; the building has a 120/240-volt, single-phase electrical system. What MINIMUM size copper conductors with THHN/THWN insulation are required for the
ungrounded service-lateral conductors?

A. 400 kcmil
B. 350 kcmil
C. 300 kcmil
D. 500 kcmil

2. Given: A commercial building is to be supplied from a transformer having a 480Y/277-volt, 3-phase primary and a 208Y/120-volt, 3-phase secondary. The secondary will have a balanced computed demand load of 416 amperes per phase. The transformer is required to have a MINIMUM kVA rating
of _____.

A. 100 kVA
B. 150 kVA
C. 86 kVA
D. 200 kVA

3. Manhole covers shall be OVER _____ or otherwise require the use of tools to open.

A. 25 lbs.
B. 50 lbs.
C. 75 lbs.
D. 100 lbs.

4. The branch circuit conductors supplying one or more units of information technology equipment shall have an ampacity of NOT less than _____ of the connected load.

A. 80 percent
B. 100 percent
C. 115 percent
D. 125 percent

5. In regard to a 7½ hp, 480-volt, 3-phase ac motor with an 80 percent power factor and a full-load ampere rating of 19 amperes indicated on the nameplate, and a service factor of 1.15; when the initial setting of the overload device you have selected is not sufficient to carry the load, what is the MAXIMUM setting permitted for the overload protection?

A. 21.85 amperes
B. 23.75 amperes
C. 24.70 amperes
D. 26.60 amperes

6. Electrical services and feeders for recreational vehicle parks shall be calculated on the basis of NOT less than _____ per RV site equipped with both 20-ampere and 30-ampere supply facilities.

A. 9600 volt-amperes
B. 4800 volt-amperes
C. 3600 volt-amperes
D. 2400 volt-amperes

7. What MINIMUM voltage is required after 1½ hours to serve emergency lighting from a storage battery, when the normal source voltage of 120 volts is interrupted?

A. 60 volts
B. 90 volts
C. 105 volts
D. 120 volts

8. Determine the absolute MAXIMUM ampere setting permitted for an overload protective device responsive to motor current, where used to protect a 20 hp, 240-volt, 3-phase, induction type ac motor with a temperature rise of 48 deg. C and a FLA of 54 amperes indicated on the nameplate.

A. 54.0 amperes
B. 70.2 amperes
C. 62.1 amperes
D. 75.6 amperes

9. Where Type SRD multiconductor cable consist of size 8 AWG conductors and only two (2) conductors in the cable are current-carrying, what is the allowable ampacity of the conductors?

A. 20 amperes
B. 30 amperes
C. 40 amperes
D. 50 amperes

10. Aluminum or steel cable trays shall be permitted to be used as equipment grounding conductors, provided _____.

     I. the cable tray sections and fittings are identified as an equipment grounding conductor
     II. the cable tray sections and fittings are durably marked to show the cross-sectional area of the metal

A. I only
B. II only
C. neither I nor II
D. both I and II

11. When intermediate metal conduit (IMC) is threaded in the field, a standard cutting die with a _____ taper per ft. shall be used.

A. 3/8 in.
B. 1/2 in.
C. 3/4 in.
D. 1 in.

12. In regard to emergency systems, where internal combustion engines are used as the prime movers, they shall NOT be solely dependent on a public utility gas system for their fuel supply, unless _____.

A. it is acceptable to the authority having jurisdiction
B. the gas system is listed and approved
C. the gas system and electrical utility are jointly owned and maintained
D. none of these apply

13. When a motor controller enclosure is installed outdoors and is subject to be exposed to sleet, it shall have a MINIMUM rating of _____, where the controller mechanism is required to be operable when ice covered.

A. Type 3
B. Type 3S
C. Type 3R
D. Type 3SX

14. Each operating room of a health care facility shall be provided with a MINIMUM of _____ "hospital grade" receptacles.

A. 12
B. 24
C. 36
D. 18

15. Ceiling-suspended luminaires (lighting fixtures) or paddle fans located _____ or more above the maximum water level of an indoor installed spa or hot tub shall NOT require GFCI protection.

A. 10 feet
B. 7½ feet
C. 8 feet
D. 12 feet

16. When flat conductor cable (FCC) is used for general-purpose branch circuits, the MAXIMUM rating of the circuits shall be _____.

A. 20 amperes
B. 30 amperes
C. 15 amperes
D. 10 amperes

17. When sizing overcurrent protection for fire pump motors, the device(s) shall be selected or set to carry indefinitely the _____ of the motor.

A. starting current
B. full-load running current
C. locked-rotor current
D. full-load amperage as indicated on the nameplate

18. Under which, if any, of the following conditions is the neutral conductor to be counted as a current-carrying conductor?

   I. When it is only carrying the unbalanced current.
   II. When it is the neutral conductor of a 3-phase, wye-connected system that consist of nonlinear loads.

A. I only
B. II only
C. neither I nor II
D. both I and II

19. In general, all mechanical elements used to terminate a grounding electrode conductor or bonding jumper to a grounding electrode shall be accessible. Which of the following, if any, is/are an exception(s) to this rule?

   I. A connection to a concrete encased electrode.
   II. A compression connection to fire-proofed structural metal.

A. I only
B. II only
C. neither I nor II
D. both I and II

20. For other than listed low-voltage luminaires not requiring grounding, all electrical equipment within a fountain or within _____ of the inside wall of a fountain shall be grounded.

A. 5 feet
B. 6 feet
C. 8 feet
D. 10 feet

21. Fuses shall NOT be permitted to be connected in parallel where _____.

   I. they are factory assembled and listed as a unit
   II. they are installed by a technician on the jobsite

A. I only
B. II only
C. neither I nor II
D. both I and II

22. Each multiwire branch circuit shall be provided with a means that will _____ at the point where the branch circuit originates.

A. simultaneously disconnect all ungrounded conductors
B. not simultaneously disconnect all ungrounded conductors
C. simultaneously disconnect all grounded and ungrounded conductors
D. simultaneously disconnect all grounded, ungrounded and grounding
   conductors

23. When calculating the total load for a mobile home park before demand factors are taken into consideration, each individual mobile home lot shall be calculated at a MINIMMUM of _____.

A. 20,000 VA
B. 15,000 VA
C. 24,000 VA
D. 16,000 VA

24. A single electrode consisting of a ground rod, pipe, or plate that does not have a resistance to ground of 25 ohms or less, shall be supplemented by one (1) additional electrode. Which of the following listed is/are approved for this purpose?

A. a concrete-encased electrode
B. a ground ring
C. the metal frame of the building
D. all of these

25. It shall be permissible to compute the feeder and service loads for dwellings using the optional method of calculations for dwellings instead of the general method of calculations for dwellings, if the dwelling unit is supplied with a single-phase, 120/240-volt service and the load is at LEAST _____ or greater.

A. 100 amperes
B. 125 amperes
C. 200 amperes
D. 150 amperes

26. In the critical care (Category 1) spaces of a health care facility, each patient bed location shall be provided with a MINIMUM of _____ ” hospital grade” receptacles.

A. fourteen
B. twelve
C. ten
D. eight

27. Nonmetallic surface extensions shall be permitted to be run in any direction from an existing outlet, but NOT within _____ of the floor level.

A. 1 foot
B. 1½ feet
C. 2 feet
D. 2 inches

28. The NEC® permits a building to have more than one service when:

I. the load requirements of the building are at least in excess of 800 amperes.
II. the building is separated by firewalls with a four-hour rating.

A. I only
B. II only
C. either I or II
D. neither I nor II

29. In the garage of a dwelling unit, a 125-volt, single-phase, 15 amperes, receptacle installed in the ceiling provided for the garage door opener must be _____.

I. a single receptacle
II. GFCI protected for personnel

A. I only
B. II only
C. either I or II
D. neither I nor II

30. Underground installed service conductors that are not encased in concrete and buried 18 inches or more below grade level, shall have their location identified by a warning ribbon placed at LEAST _____ above the underground installation.

A. 6 inches
B. 8 inches
C. 12 inches
D. 18 inches

31. Outlets supplying permanently installed swimming pool pump motors from single-phase, 15- or 20-ampere, 120- or 240-volt branch circuits, shall be provided with GFCI protection _____.

A. where installed outdoors
B. when cord-and-plug connected
C. when direct (hard-wired) connected
D. where any of the above conditions exist

32. The branch circuit conductors supplying a 240-volt, single-phase, 15 kW rated fixed electric space heater provided with a 10-ampere blower motor are required to have an ampacity of at LEAST _____.

A. 63 amperes
B. 78 amperes
C. 91 amperes
D. 109 amperes

33. A commercial kitchen is to contain the following listed cooking related equipment:

   * one - 14 kW range
   * one - 5.0 kW water heater
   * one - 0.75 kW mixer
   * one - 2.5 kW dishwasher
   * one - 2.0 kW booster heater
   * one - 2.0 kW broiler

Determine the demand load, in kW, after applying the demand factors for the kitchen equipment.

A. 19.00 kW
B. 26.25 kW
C. 18.38 kW
D. 17.06 kW

34. When two (2) ground rods are used to form the entire grounding electrode system of a building, the grounding conductor that bonds the two rods together shall NOT be required to be larger than size _____ copper, regardless of the size of the service-entrance conductors.

A. 8 AWG
B. 6 AWG
C. 4 AWG
D. 2 AWG

35. A kitchen with a total demand load of 54,000 VA is to be added to an existing church. The electrical system is 208Y/120-volts, 3-phase. What MINIMUM size THWN copper feeder conductors are required for the kitchen addition?

A. 1 AWG
B. 1/0 AWG
C. 2/0 AWG
D. 3/0 AWG

36. A feeder at a school welding shop is to supply the following listed transformer arc welders all with a 50 percent duty cycle.

   * two (2) with 60 amperes rated primary current
   * two (2) with 50 amperes rated primary current
   * two (2) with 40 amperes rated primary current

The feeder is required to have an ampacity of at LEAST _____.

A. 213 amperes
B. 196 amperes
C. 182 amperes
D. 176 amperes

37. The National Electrical Code® requires ventilation of a battery room where batteries are being charged to prevent:

A. battery corrosion.
B. electrostatic charge.
C. deterioration of the building steel.
D. an accumulation of an explosive mixture.

38. What is the MAXIMUM balanced demand load, in VA, permitted to be connected to a new service of a commercial building, given the following conditions?

   I. The service is 208Y/120 volts, 3-phase, with a 600-ampere rated main circuit breaker.
   II. The maximum load must not exceed 80 percent of the ampere rating of the main circuit breaker.

A. 57,600 VA
B. 99,840 VA
C. 172,923 VA
D. 178,692 VA

39. Determine the MAXIMUM standard size overcurrent protection required for the primary and secondary side of a transformer, when primary and secondary overcurrent protection is to be provided, given the following related information.

   * 150 kVA rating
   * Primary - 480 volt, 3-phase, 3-wire
   * Secondary - 208Y/120 volt, 3-phase, 4-wire

A. Primary - 500 amperes, Secondary - 500 amperes
B. Primary - 450 amperes, Secondary - 600 amperes
C. Primary - 500 amperes, Secondary - 450 amperes
D. Primary - 450 amperes, Secondary - 500 amperes

40. Openings around electrical penetrations of a wall of a designated information technology room are required to be _____.

A. insulated
B. airtight
C. firestopped
D. soundproof

41. When buried raceways pass under streets, roads or driveways, the MINIMUM cover requirements _____.

A. decrease if installed in rigid metal conduit (RMC)
B. do not change in regard to wiring methods used
C. shall be increased for direct burial cables
D. can be increased, decreased, or remain the same, depending on the wiring method used

42. For capacitors over 1000 volts, a means shall be provided to reduce the residual voltage to _____ after the capacitor is disconnected from the source of power.

A. 50 volts or less within 1 minute
B. 50 volts or less within 5 minutes
C. 24 volts or less within 5 minutes
D. 12 volts or less within 1 minute

43. Where used outside of a, building, aluminum or copper-clad aluminum grounding electrode conductors shall not be terminated WITHIN_____ of the earth.

A. 18 inches
B. 24 inches
C. 3 feet
D. 6 feet

44. Where installed for a commercial occupancy, determine the MINIMUM size THWN copper conductors required from the terminals of a 3-phase, 277/480-volt, 4-wire, 200 kW generator to the first distribution device(s) containing overcurrent protection. Assume the design and operation of the generator does NOT prevent overloading.

A. 250 kcmil
B. 300 kcmil
C. 400 kcmil
D. 500 kcmil

45. Enclosures containing circuit breakers, switches and motor controllers located in Class II, Division 2 locations, shall be _____ or otherwise identified for the location.

A. gastight
B. vapor-proof
C. dusttight
D. stainless steel

46. Information technology equipment is permitted to be connected to a branch circuit by flexible cord-and-attachment plug cap, if the cord does NOT
exceed _____ in length.

A. 6 feet
B. 8 feet
C. 10 feet
D. 15 feet

47. Where required, conduit seals installed in Class I, Division 1 & 2 locations shall have the minimum thickness of the sealing compound not less than the trade size of the sealing fitting and, in no case less than _____.

A. 1/2 in.
B. 5/8 in.
C. 3/4 in.
D. 1 in.

48. Given: A one-family dwelling to be built will have 4,000 sq. ft. of livable space, a 600 sq. ft. garage, a 400 sq. ft. open porch, a 2,000 sq. ft. unfinished basement (adaptable for future use), three (3) small-appliance branch-circuits and a branch circuit for the laundry room. Determine the demand load, in VA, on the ungrounded service-entrance conductors for the general lighting and receptacle loads using the standard method of calculation for a one-family dwelling.

A. 10,350 VA
B. 9,825 VA
C. 7,350 VA
D. 24,000 VA

49. Determine the MINIMUM size Type SOW flexible cord that may be used to supply a 30 hp, 3-phase, 480-volt, continuous-duty, ac motor from the motor controller to the motor terminations. Assume voltage-drop and elevated ambient temperature are not considerations.

A. 4 AWG
B. 6 AWG
C. 8 AWG
D. 10 AWG

50. Portable structures for fairs, carnivals and similar events shall not be located under or within _____ horizontally of conductors operating in excess of 600 volts.

A. 22½ feet
B. 15 feet
C. 10 feet
D. 12 feet

51. Flexible cord and cables shall be permitted to be attached to building surfaces _____.

A. under no circumstances
B. where concealed
C. where used as a substitute for the fixed wiring of a structure
D. where the length of the cord or cable from a busway plug-in device to a suitable tension "take-up" support device does not exceed 6 feet

52. In regard to outside branch circuits of overhead spans of open individual conductors for 1000 volts or less up to 50 feet in length, the NEC® mandates the conductors to be NOT less than _____ copper in size.

A. 12 AWG
B. 10 AWG
C. 8 AWG
D. 6 AWG

53. The ampacity requirements for a disconnecting means of x-ray equipment shall be based on at LEAST _____ of the input required for the momentary rating of the equipment, if greater than the long-term rating.

A. 125 percent
B. 115 percent
C. 80 percent
D. 50 percent

54. The MINIMUM spacing required between live bare metal parts in feeder circuits of 480-volt industrial control panels and bare metal parts of the enclosure is _____.

A. 1/2 in.
B. 3/4 in.
C. 1 in.
D. 1¼ in.

55. AFCI protection is required for all 15- and 20-ampere, 120-volt branch circuits supplying outlets located in _____.

A. boat houses
B. recreational vehicles
C. all guest rooms and suites of hotels
D. residential garages

56. All swimming pool electric water heaters shall have the heating elements subdivided into loads not exceeding 48 amperes and protected at NOT over _____ .

A. 45 amperes
B. 50 amperes
C. 55 amperes
D. 60 amperes

57. In regard to emergency and legally required standby systems, transfer switches shall be _____ and approved by the authority having jurisdiction.

A. manual
B. automatic
C. nonautomatic
D. red in color

58. Where Type SE service-entrance cable with ungrounded conductors' sizes 10 AWG or smaller, is used for interior wiring as a substitute for Type NM cable, is installed in thermal insulation, the ampacity shall be in accordance with the _____ conductor temperature rating.

A. 40°C
B. 60°C
C. 75°C
D. 90°C

59. Power distribution blocks shall be permitted in pull and junction boxes having a volume over _____ for connections of conductors where installed in boxes, provided the power distribution blocks do not have uninsulated live parts exposed within the box, whether or not the box cover is exposed.

A. 50 cu. in.
B. 75 cu. in.
C. 100 cu. in.
D. 1650 cu. in.

60. Where a receptacle outlet is removed from an underfloor raceway, the conductors supplying the outlet shall be _____ .

A. capped with an approved insulating material
B. taped off with red colored tape
C. marked and identified
D. removed from the raceway

61. What is the MINIMUM dimension required by the NEC® for a working space containing live parts on both sides of the equipment that will require
examination and maintenance of the equipment when energized and operating at 480-volts between conductors?

A. 4 feet
B. 3 feet
C. 6 feet
D. 5 feet

62. Where a mobile home park has 25 mobile home lots calculated at 15,000 VA for each mobile home, determine the MINIMUM required ampacity required for the ungrounded service-entrance conductors.

A. 400 amperes
B. 380 amperes
C. 820 amperes
D. 782 amperes

63. A 3-phase, 150 kVA transformer with a 208Y/120-volt secondary has an existing load of 212 amperes on each of the ungrounded phases. What is the MAXIMUM load, in amperes, that may be added to each of the ungrounded secondary phases?

A. 416 amperes
B. 180 amperes
C. 204 amperes
D. 250 amperes

64. In regard to an isolated grounding type receptacle, the reason the insulated isolated grounding conductor is not bonded to the outlet box is _____.

A. for the reduction of electrical noise
B. to insure the circuit breaker will trip in the event of a ground-fault
C. to prevent the circuit breaker from tripping in the event of a ground-fault
D. for the reduction of voltage-drop

65. Where a central vacuum assembly is located in a storage closet adjacent to the laundry room of a dwelling, accessible non-current-carrying metal parts of the assembly likely to be energized shall be _____.

A. isolated
B. insulated
C. GFCI protected
D. connected to an equipment grounding conductor

66. Type CMP communications cable of NOT more than _____ in length shall be permitted in ducts used for environmental air if they are directly associated with the air distribution system.

A. 8 feet
B. 6 feet
C. 4 feet
D. 2 feet

67. The disconnecting switch or circuit breaker for electric signs and outline lighting systems shall open all _____ conductors simultaneously on multi-wire branch circuits supplying the sign or outline lighting system.

A. grounded and ungrounded
B. grounded, ungrounded and grounding
C. grounding, ungrounded and bonding
D. ungrounded

68. In an industrial establishment, what is the MAXIMUM length of 200 ampere rated busway that may be tapped to a 600-ampere rated busway, without additional overcurrent protection?

A. 10 feet
B. 25 feet
C. 50 feet
D. 75 feet

69. For circuits of OVER _____ to ground, the electrical continuity of rigid metal conduit (RMC) or intermediate metal conduit (IMC) that contain any conductor other than service conductors shall be insured with two (2) locknuts, one inside and one outside the box or cabinet.

A. 480 volts
B. 300 volts
C. 250 volts
D. 125 volts

70. In general, the NEC® does not mandate the maximum number of circuit breakers a panelboard may contain. An exception to this rule is _____, which is limited to no more than 42 overcurrent protection devices.

A. a delta-connected panelboard
B. a split-bus panelboard
C. a 3-phase panelboard
D. panelboards containing overcurrent protection devices rated only 30
   amperes or less

71. When water reaches the height of the established electrical datum plane for an irrigation pond, the service equipment must _____.

A. be installed in a NEMA 6 enclosure
B. float
C. be installed in a NEMA 6P enclosure
D. disconnect

72. In health care facilities, essential electrical systems shall have a MINIMUM _____.

A. capacity of 200 gallons of fuel for the auxiliary generator
B. of two independent sources of power
C. of 1-hour back-up time
D. capacity of 150 kVA

73. Lampholders shall be constructed, installed, or equipped with shades or guards so that combustible material is not subjected to temperatures in EXCESS of _____.

A. 130 degrees F
B. 140 degrees F
C. 162 degrees F
D. 194 degrees F

74. Pendant conductors having a length of at LEAST _____ or more, shall be twisted together where not cabled in a listed assembly.

A. 3 feet
B. 4 feet
C. 5 feet
D. 6 feet

75. For nonshielded conductors of over 1000 volts, the conductors shall NOT be bent to a radius of less than _____ times the overall conductor material.

A. six
B. eight
C. ten
D. twelve

76. At least one structural support member of a building or structure that is direct contact with the earth for at LEAST _____ or more, with or without concrete encasement shall be permitted to be used as a grounding electrode.

A. 20 feet
B. 8 feet
C. 10 feet
D. 6 feet

77. The circuit supplying an autotransformer-type dimmer installed in theaters and similar places shall NOT exceed _____ between conductors.

A. 480 volts
B. 277 volts
C. 250 volts
D. 150 volts

78. At least one 125-volt, single-phase 15- or 20-ampere rated receptacle outlet shall be installed within 18 inches of the top of a show window of a retail store for each _____ of show window area measured horizontally.

A. 8 linear ft.
B. 10 linear ft.
C. 12 linear ft.
D. 15 linear ft.

79. Each luminaire installed in Class III, Divisions 1 and 2 locations shall be clearly marked to show the maximum wattage of the lamps that shall be permitted without exceeding an exposed surface temperature of _____ under normal conditions of use.

A. 329º F
B. 165º F
C. 144º F
D. 125º F

80. Conductors supplying a continuous-rated, varying-duty motor shall have an ampacity of NOT less than _____ of the motor nameplate current rating.

A. 125 percent
B. 140 percent
C. 150 percent
D. 200 percent

81. Where located in Class I, Division 1 locations, transformers containing oil or a liquid that will burn shall be _____.

A. enclosed in a fence
B. installed in vaults only
C. identified for use in Class I locations
D. installed in a fire-resistant room

82. Where a lighting track is installed with two (2), four (4) ft. sections, mounted end-to-end, how many supports are required?

A. five
B. four
C. three
D. two

83. What is the MAXIMUM standard size circuit breaker that may be used for overcurrent protection of size 4/0 AWG THWN copper conductors that are not serving a motor load?

A. 200 amperes
B. 225 amperes
C. 230 amperes
D. 250 amperes

84. Motor fuel dispensing systems shall be provided with one or more identified emergency shutoff devices or electrical disconnects. Such devices or disconnects shall NOT be more than _____ from the fuel dispensing units that they serve.

A. 30 feet
B. 50 feet
C. 75 feet
D. 100 feet

85. The depth of the working space in front of a 120-volt, single-phase, fire alarm control panel (FACP) is required to be at LEAST _____.

A. 2½ feet
B. 3 feet
C. 3½ feet
D. 4 feet

86. Where an air conditioning unit is supplied with size 6 AWG CU conductors and protected by a 60-ampere circuit breaker, the MINIMUM size CU equipment grounding conductor permitted for this installation is _____.

A. 12 AWG
B. 10 AWG
C. 8 AWG
D. 6 AWG

87. Which of the following is NOT required to be marked on the nameplate of a transformer?

A. overcurrent protection
B. manufacturer
C. kVA rating
D. voltage

88. When combination surface nonmetallic raceways are used for both signaling and for power and lighting circuits, the different systems shall be _____.

A. prohibited
B. run in the same compartment
C. run in separate compartments
D. maintain a spacing of at least ½ in.

89. Where explosionproof equipment is provided with metric threaded entries, which of the following methods is approved to adapt the entries from metric threads to NPT threads?

A. Approved adapters from metric threads to NPT threads shall be used.
B. Tap the metric threaded entries to NPT threads.
C. Thread the conduit with metric threads.
D. All of these are approved methods.

90. Where installed outdoors, dry-type transformers exceeding 112½ kVA shall NOT be located within _____ of combustible materials of buildings, unless the transformer has Class 155 insulation systems or higher and completely enclosed except for ventilating openings.

A. 6 inches
B. 10 inches
C. 12 inches
D. 18 inches

91. A clearance of NOT less than _____ must be maintained from the maximum water level of a permanently installed swimming pool and messenger-supported *tri-plex* service-drop conductors of 0-750 volts.

A. 10 feet
B. 14½ feet
C. 19 feet
D. 22½ feet

92. Where an apartment complex has a calculated connected lighting load of 205.4 kVA, what is the DEMAND load, in kVA, on the ungrounded service-entrance conductors where applying the standard (general) method of calculation? Given: Each dwelling unit in the complex has cooking facilities provided.

A. 58.9 kVA
B. 60.2 kVA
C. 16.5 kVA
D. 65.3 kVA

93. What is the MINIMUM permitted sill height of a transformer vault doorway?

A. 2 inches
B. 4 inches
C. 6 inches
D. 8 inches

94. For the purpose of sizing branch circuits for fixed storage-type water heaters with a capacity of 120 gallons or less, the water heater shall be considered _____.

A. a continuous load
B. an intermittent load
C. a noncontinuous load
D. a short-time load

95. When supplying a 36,000 VA, 240-volt, single-phase load in an area where the ambient temperature reaches 119º F, determine the MINIMUM size 75ºC rated copper conductors required to supply the load.

A. 1/0 AWG
B. 2/0 AWG
C. 3/0 AWG
D. 4/0 AWG

96. Color coding shall be permitted to identify intrinsically safe conductors where they are colored _____ and where no other conductors of the same color are used.

A. light blue
B. orange
C. yellow
D. purple

97. What is the MINIMUM bend radius of trade size 4 in. rigid metal conduit (RMC) where the bend is not made with a one-shot or full-shoe bender?

A. 16 inches
B. 18 inches
C. 24 inches
D. 30 inches

98. Where exceptions are not to be applied, determine the MINIMUM required length of a junction box that has a trade size 3½ in. conduit containing four (4) size 250 kcmil conductors, pulled through the box for a 90º angle pull.

A. 21 inches
B. 24 inches
C. 28 inches
D. 34 inches

99. An approved method of protection for equipment installed in Class I, Zone 0, hazardous locations are _____.

A. purged and pressurized
B. encapsulation
C. powder filling
D. oil immersion

100. Cables operating at over 1000 volts and those operating at 1000 volts or less, are permitted to be installed in a common cable tray without a fixed barrier, where the cables operating at over 1000 volts are _____.

A. Type MI
B. Type AC
C. Type CT
D. Type MC

Please See Answer Key on following page

ALH 04/03/2019

1Exam Prep
NFPA 70 National Electrical Code, 2017
Final Exam 1
Questions and Answers

ANSWER KEY

Answer	Section/Page#

1. D

300.5(B)
Table 310.104(A)
Table 310.15(B)(16)
Single-phase Current Formula

$I = P \div E$ $I = 90,000$ VA $\div 240$ volts $= 375$ amperes

Size 500 kcmil THHN/THWN conductors with an ampacity of 380 amperes should be selected from Table 310.15(B)(16).

2. B

3-phase Power Formula
VA = I x E x 1.732

VA = 416 amperes x 208 volts x 1.732 = 149,866 VA
149,866 VA ÷ 1,000 = 149.8 kVA

3. D   110.75(D)

4. D   645.5(A)

5. D   430.6(A)(2)
              430.32(A)(1)
              430.32(C)

19 amperes x 140% = 26.60 amperes

6. C   551.73(A)

7. C   700.12(A)

120 volts x 87.5% = 105 volts

8. B   430.6(A)(2)
              430.32(C)

54 amperes x 130% = 70.2 amperes

Answer	**Section/Page#**
9. C	Table 440.5(A)(1), Column B
10. D	392.60(B)(1) & (3)
11. C	342.28
12. A	700.12(B)(3), Exception
13. B	Table 110.28
14. C	517.19(C)(1)
15. D	680.43(B)(1)(a)
16. A	324.10(B)(2)
17. C	695.5(B)
18. B	310.15(B)(5)(a) &(c)
19. D	250.68(A), Exceptions 1 & 2
20. A	680.54(1)
21. B	240.8
22. A	210.4(B)
23. D	550.31(1)
24. D	250.53(A)(2) 250.52(A)(2) -(A)(8)
25. A	220.82(A)
26. A	517.19(B)(1)
27. D	382.15(A)
28. D	230.2(A), (B), &(C)
29. B	210.8(A)(2)
30. C	300.5(D)(3)
31. D	680.21(C)

Answer	Section/Page#

32. C
424.3(B)
210.19(A)(1)(a)
Single-Phase Current Formula

$$I = \frac{kW \times 1,000}{volts} \quad I = \frac{15 \times 1,000}{240} = \frac{15,000}{240} = 62.5 \text{ amperes (heater)}$$

```
  62.5 amperes (heater)
+ 10.0 amperes (blower)
  72.5 amperes x 125% = 91 amperes
```

33. A
220.56
Table 220.56

```
14.00 kW - range
 5.00 kW - water heater
 0.75 kW - mixer
 2.50 kW - dishwasher
 2.00 kW - booster heater
 2.00 kW - broiler
26.25 kW - total connected load x 65% = 17.06 kW
```

*NOTE: However, the NEC® states the demand shall not be less than the two largest pieces of equipment. 14.00 kW + 5.00 kW = 19 kW demand

34. B
250.66(A)

35. B
3-phase current formula
Table 310.15(B)(16)

$$I = \frac{54,000 \text{ VA}}{208 \times 1.732} = \frac{54,000}{360.25} = 149.89 \text{ amperes}$$

Size 1/0 THWN conductors with an ampacity of 150 amperes should be selected from Table 310.15(B)(16).

36. D
Table 630.11(A)
630.11(B)

```
60 amperes x .71 = 43 amperes x 100% =  43 amperes
60 amperes x .71 = 43 amperes x 100% =  43 amperes
50 amperes x .71 = 36 amperes x 85%  =  31 amperes
50 amperes x .71 = 36 amperes x 70%  =  25 amperes
40 amperes x .71 = 28 amperes x 60%  =  17 amperes
40 amperes x .71 = 28 amperes x 60%  =  17 amperes
                          TOTAL  = 176 amperes
```

Answer	Section/Page#

37. D   480.10(A)

38. C   3-phase Power Formula
$P = I \times E \times 1.732$

$P = 600$ amperes $\times 208$ volts $\times 1.732 \times 80\% = 172,923$ VA

39. B   3-phase Current Formula
450.3(B)
Table 450.3(B)
Table 240.6(A)

(Primary)
$I = \dfrac{kVA \times 1,000}{E \times 1.732}$ $I = \dfrac{150 \times 1,000}{480 \times 1.732} = \dfrac{150,000}{831.36} = 180$ amps $\times 250\% = 450$ amps

(Secondary)
$I = \dfrac{kVA \times 1,000}{E \times 1.732}$ $I = \dfrac{150 \times 1,000}{208 \times 1.732} = \dfrac{150,000}{360.25} = 416$ amps $\times 125\% = 520$ amps

*NOTE: For the secondary you are permitted to go up to the next standard
size overcurrent device which has a rating of 600 amperes.

40. C   645.3(A)
300.21

41. B   Table 300.5

42. B   460.28(A)

43. A   250.64(A)

44. B   3-phase Current Formula
445.13(A)
Table 310.15(B)(16)

$I = \dfrac{kW \times 1,000}{volts \times 1.732}$ $I = \dfrac{200 \times 1,000}{480 \times 1.732} = \dfrac{200,000}{831.36} = 240.56$ amperes (FLC)

241 amperes $\times 115\% = 277$ amperes (required ampacity of conductors)

Size 300 kcmil THWN conductors with an allowable ampacity of 285
amperes should be selected.

45. C   502.115(B)

46. D   645.5(B)(1)

Answer	Section/Page#
47. B	501.15(C)(3)
48. A	220.12
	Table 220.12
	220.52(A) & (B)
	Table 220.42

4,000 sq. ft. + 2,000 sq. ft. = 6,000 sq. ft. x 3 VA = 18,000 VA
three small appliance circuits @ 1,500 VA each   =   4,500 VA
one laundry circuit @ 1,500 VA   =   <u>1,500 VA</u>
                 Total connected load   = 24,000 VA

1st 3,000 VA @ 100%   3,000 VA
24,000 VA - 3,000 VA = 21,000 VA (remainder) @ 35% = 7,350 <u>VA</u>
                   Total demand load   = 10,350 VA

49. A	430.6 & .6(A)(1)
	430.22
	Table 430.250
	Table 400.5(A)(1), Column A

FLC of 30 HP motor = 40 amperes x 125% = 50 amperes

     Size 4 AWG SOW cord with an allowable ampacity of 60 amperes should
     be selected from Table 400.5(A)(1).

50. B	525.5(B)(2)
51. D	400.12(4), Exception
	368.56(B)(2)
52. B	225.6(A)(1)
53. D	517.72(A)
54. C	409.106
	Table 430.97(D)
55. C	210.12(A)
	210.12(C)
56. D	680.10
57. B	700.5(A)
	701.5(A)
58. B	338.10(B)(4)(a)

Answer	Section/Page#
59. C	314.28(E)
60. D	390.8
61. A	Table 110.26(A)(1), Condition 3

62. A   550.30 & .31(1)
Table 550.31
Single-phase current formula

25 lots x 16,000 VA (minimum) = 400,000 VA
$$\underline{\text{X .24}} \quad \text{(demand factor)}$$
96,000 VA (demand load)

$I = \dfrac{\text{power}}{\text{Volts}}$ $I = \dfrac{96,000 \text{ VA}}{240 \text{ volts}} = 400$ amperes

63. C   3-phase current formula

$I = \dfrac{\text{kVA x 1000}}{\text{E x 1.732}}$ $I = \dfrac{150 \times 1000}{208 \times 1.732} = \dfrac{150,000}{360.25} = 416$ amperes (FLA)

                                                  - $\underline{212 \text{ amperes}}$ (existing load)
                                                 = 204 amperes (additional load)

64. A	250.146(D)
65. D	422.15(C)
66. C	800.113(B)(1)
67. D	600.6
68. C	368.17(B), Exception
69. C	250.97(2)
70. B	408.36, Exception 2
71. D	682.11
72. B	517.30(A)
73. D	410.97
74. A	410.54(C)
75. B	300.34
76. C	250.52(A)(2)

Answer	Section/Page#
77. D	520.25(C)
78. C	210.62
79. A	503.130(A)
80. D	430.22(E) Table 430.22(E)
81. B	501.100(A)(1)
82. C	410.154
83. D	Table 310.15(B)(16) 240.4(B)(2) & (3) Table 240.6(A)
84. D	514.11(A)
85. B	Table 110.26(A)(1)
86. B	Table 250.122
87. A	450.11(A)
88. C	388.70
89. A	500.8(E)(2)
90. C	450.22(A)
91. D	Table 680.9(A)
92. D	Table 220.42

205.4 kVA x 1,000 = 205,400 VA

first 3,000 VA @ 100%	= 3,000 VA
3,001 to 120,000 VA @ 35% = 117,000 VA @ 35%	= 40,950 VA
Remainder 205,400 VA – 120,000 VA = 85,400 VA @ 25% =	21,350 VA
Demand	= 65,300 VA

$$\frac{65,300 \text{ VA}}{1,000} = 65.3 \text{ kVA}$$

93. B	450.43(B)
94. A	422.13

<u>Answer</u>	<u>Section/Page#</u>

95. C   Single-phase current formula
         Table 310.15(B)(16)
         Table 310.15(B)(2)(a)

$$I = \frac{power}{volts} \qquad I = \frac{36,000 \text{ VA}}{240 \text{ volts}} = 150 \text{ amperes load}$$

$$required \; ampacity = \frac{150 \text{ amperes}}{.75 \text{ (temp. cor.)}} = 200 \text{ amperes}$$

96. A   504.80(C)

97. C   Chapter 9, Table 2

98. A   314.28(A)(2)

         3.5 inches (conduit) x 6 = 21 inches

99. B   505.8(G)

100. D   392.20(B)(1)

NFPA 70 National Electrical Code, 2017
Final Exam 2

1. For individual dwelling units with single-phase, 120/240-volt electrical systems of not over 400 amperes, the NEC® permits the service conductors to have an ampacity NOT less than _____ of the service rating.

A. 80%
B. 83%
C. 75%
D. 70%

2. Where multiple driven ground rods, driven pipes or buried plate grounding electrodes are installed to meet the rules set forth by the NEC®, the electrodes shall NOT be spaced less than _____ apart.

A. 6 feet
B. 8 feet
C. 4 feet
D. 5 feet

3. When an ac general-use snap switch is used as a controller for a single-phase, 2 hp, 240-volt, ac motor, the switch is required to have a rating of at LEAST_____.

A. 10 amperes
B. 15 amperes
C. 20 amperes
D. 30 amperes

4. Conductors shall be permitted to be tapped to feeder conductors without overcurrent protection at the tap where the length of the tap conductors does not exceed 25 feet. However, the tap conductors are to have an ampacity of NOT less than _____ of the ampacity of the feeder conductors to which they are tapped.

A. one-fourth
B. one-half
C. three-quarters
D. one-third

5. A circuit breaker that serves as both the disconnecting means and as a controller for a motor is required to be _____.

I. marked SWD
II. rated 30 amperes or less

A. I only
B. II only
C. both I and II
D. neither I nor II

6. Which of the following listed is NOT a requirement for an intersystem bonding termination?

A. Consist of not less than three (3) terminals.
B. Connected to the meter enclosure only with a minimum size 8 AWG conductor.
C. Terminals shall be listed for grounding and bonding.
D. Be accessible for connection and inspection.

7. Polyvinyl chloride conduit (PVC) larger than trade size _____ shall not be used.

A. 4 inch
B. 5 inch
C. 4½ inch
D. 6 inch

8. Nonmetallic sheathed cable, Type NM, is permitted to enter the top of surface-mounted cabinets and boxes through nonflexible raceways not less than 18 inches or more than _____ in length, provided all the mandated conditions are met.

A. four feet
B. eight feet
C. six feet
D. ten feet

9. Flat cable assemblies (Type FC) shall be permitted for use as:

A. feeder circuits.
B. branch circuits not exceeding 30 amperes.
C. branch circuits not exceeding 20 amperes.
D. feeder or branch circuits not to exceed 50 amperes.

10. Where a building or structure is supplied with a 3-phase, 480Y/277-volt electrical system, each disconnecting means rated at LEAST _____ or more shall be provided with ground-fault protection.

A. 800 amperes
B. 1,200 amperes
C. 1,000 amperes
D. 1,500 amperes

11. Exposed power-limited fire alarm (PLFA) circuit conductors shall be protected from physical damage up to _____ above the floor.

A. 6 feet
B. 8 feet
C. 10 feet
D. 7 feet

12. A fused disconnecting means for a 3-phase, 480-volt motor shall have an ampere rating of NOT less than _____ of the full-load current rating of the motor.

A. 115 percent
B. 125 percent
C. 150 percent
D. 175 percent

13. A MINIMUM separation between heating elements of electric space-heating cables installed in ceilings and the edge of outlet boxes and junction boxes used for surface-mounted luminaires shall NOT be less than _____.

A. 6 inches
B. 8 inches
C. 4 inches
D. 12 inches

14. Where multiple driven ground rod electrodes make up the entire grounding electrode system for a building or structure having a 480Y/277-volt, 1,200 ampere rated service, what is the MINIMUM size copper conductor required to bond the ground rods together?

A. 8 AWG
B. 6 AWG
C. 4 AWG
D. 1/0 AWG

15. Where conduits or other raceways enter floor-standing switchboards, panelboards or switchgear from the bottom, the conduits or raceways, including their end fittings, shall not rise more than _____ above the bottom of the enclosure.

A. 4 inches
B. 6 inches
C. 2 inches
D. 3 inches

16. In regard to the size of pull and junction boxes for use on electrical systems over 1000 volts, for straight pulls, the length of the box shall NOT be less than _____ the outside diameter, over sheath, of the largest shielded or lead-covered conductor or cable entering the box.

A. 48 times
B. 36 times
C. 32 times
D. 24 times

17. In motion picture studios, television studios and similar locations, each receptacle of dc plugging boxes shall be rated NOT less than how many amperes?

A. 15 amperes
B. 20 amperes
C. 25 amperes
D. 30 amperes

18. Where sizes 1/0 AWG through 4/0 AWG single conductor cables are installed in ladder type cable tray, the MAXIMUM allowable rung spacing for the ladder type cable tray shall be _____.

A. 6 inches
B. 9 inches
C. 10 inches
D. 12 inches

19. Type UF cable is NOT permitted to be used _____.

A. as a substitute for Type NM cable
B. in an attic space
C. as service-entrance conductors
D. as single conductor cables

20. When applying the general method of calculations for dwelling units, the permitted demand factor, in percent, on the feeder and service conductors for five (5) household clothes dryers is _____.

A. 85%
B. 75%
C. 70%
D. 60%

21. Where installed in commercial occupancies or industrial facilities, the MINIMUM height (headroom) of working spaces about service equipment, switchboards, switchgear, panelboards, motor control centers and similar equipment of 1000-volts or less is _____ or the height of the equipment, whichever is greater.

A. 72 inches
B. 78 inches
C. 84 inches
D. 96 inches

22. As per the NEC®, plate grounding electrodes shall be installed NOT less than _____ below the surface of the earth.

A. 12 inches
B. 18 inches
C. 24 inches
D. 30 inches

23. Size 14 AWG branch circuit tap conductors that serve individual outlets other than receptacles, are permitted to be tapped from 20-ampere rated branch circuit conductors when the _____.

A. load on the tap conductors is not more than 10 amperes
B. load on the size 14 AWG conductors is not more than 8 amperes
C. size 14 AWG conductor length is not more than 18 inches
D. conductor length is limited to 36 inches

24. The branch-circuit, short-circuit and ground-fault protection for a hermetic motor-compressor shall have a rating or setting NOT exceeding _____ of the motor-compressor rated-load current or branch-circuit selection, whichever is greater, where the protection specified is sufficient for the starting current of the motor and modifications are not necessary.

A. 150 percent
B. 175 percent
C. 125 percent
D. 225 percent

25. Where an electrical equipment room houses large equipment that contains overcurrent protective devices or switching devices, and the equipment is 1000-volts or less, rated 1,200-amperes or more and over 6 feet wide, for the purposes of entering and exiting the working space, two (2) entrances are required, one at each end. The doors are required to be not less than 6½ ft. high and NOT less than _____ wide.

A. 2 ft.
B. 2½ ft.
C. 3 ft.
D. 3½ ft.

26. Given: A trade size 1 in. Schedule 40 PVC conduit is run horizontally out of the side of a panelboard for 50 feet, then turns at a 90° angle vertically for 40 feet where it enters the building through a LB conduit body. How many expansion fittings are required for this installation?

A. one
B. two
C. three
D. four

27. As a general rule, luminaires and lampholders shall have no live parts exposed to contact, an exception to this rule is where cleat-type lampholders are located at LEAST _____ or more above the floor, they shall be permitted to have exposed terminals.

A. 12 feet
B. 10 feet
C. 7 feet
D. 8 feet

28. What MINIMUM size 75°C copper feeder conductors are required to supply the following listed 3-phase, 230-volt, continuous-duty, ac motors?

• one (1) 15 hp wound-rotor
• one (1) 7½ hp induction-type

A. 6 AWG THHN
B. 4 AWG THHN
C. 4 AWG THWN
D. 2 AWG THW

29. AC or DC general-use snap switches may be used for control of inductive loads NOT exceeding _____ of the ampere rating of the switch at the applied voltage.

A. 50%
B. 80%
C. 60%
D. 75%

30. In general, cables or raceways shall be permitted to be laid in notches of wooden studs where the cable or raceway at those points is protected by a steel plate at LEAST _____ thick to cover the area of the wiring.

A. 1/16 in.
B. 1/8 in.
C. 1/4 in.
D. 3/8 in.

31. According to the National Electrical Code®, what would cause excessive objectionable current flow in the equipment grounding conductor when servicing an appliance branch circuit?

A. High load resistance.
B. Excessive resistance of the neutral conductor.
C. Excessive resistance of the grounding conductor.
D. Multiple connections between the neutral and grounding conductors.

32. As addressed in the NEC®, the equipotential plane in an agricultural building is an area where wire mesh or other conductive elements such as reinforcement bar are embedded in or located under concrete and bonded to _____.

A. all metal structures
B. the electrical grounding system
C. fixed nonelectrical equipment that may become energized
D. all of these

33. The NEC® recommended MAXIMUM total voltage drop on both feeders and branch circuit conductors is _____.

A. 2 percent
B. 3 percent
C. 4 percent
D. 5 percent

34. For other than single-family dwellings, an emergency disconnect switch must be provided for spas and hot tubs NOT less than _____ away from the spa or hot tub and must be readily accessible to users.

A. 6 feet
B. 10 feet
C. 5 feet
D. 12 feet

35. When normal power is lost, legally required standby systems must be able to supply standby power in at LEAST _____ or less.

A. 60 seconds
B. 10 seconds
C. 30 seconds
D. 2 minutes

36. Where conduit or tubing nipples having a length not to exceed 24 inches are installed between boxes, cabinets and similar enclosures, the nipples shall be permitted to be filled not to exceed _____ of their total cross-sectional area.

A. 40%
B. 60%
C. 70%
D. 75%

37. Receptacles supplying power to freestanding-type office furnishings shall NOT be more than _____ from the furnishing that it is connected to it.

A. 6 feet
B. 3 feet
C. 1 foot
D. 8 feet

38. A type of fuse NOT permitted for new installations and shall be used only for replacements in existing installations is a/n _____ fuse.

A. Edison-base
B. Class K
B. Class CC
D. time-delay

39. Given: An equipment disconnecting means is mounted at a height of 6 feet on a remote wall in an aircraft storage and maintenance hangar. The disconnect switch is 10 feet away from any aircraft fuel tanks. The disconnect switch is located in a/an _____ area.

A. Class II, Division 1
B. Class I, Division 2
C. Class I, Division 1
D. unclassified

40. Given: A 120/240-volt, single-phase service has a metal chain link fence opposite exposed live parts of the service equipment. The required depth of clear working space in front of the service equipment must be at LEAST _____.

A. 2 ft. 6 in.
B. 3 ft.
C. 3 ft. 6 in.
D. 4 ft.

41. Remote disconnecting controls shall NOT be required for critical operations data systems when _____.

A. an approved fire suppression system suitable for the application is in place
B. wiring is under raised floors
C. a smoke-sensing fire detection system is in place
D. both A and C

42. Given: A retail jewelry store has two (2) large show windows having a length of 15 feet each. One show window is on each side of the entry door. How many single-phase, 125-volt, 15- or 20-ampere rated receptacles must be provided for the show window lighting?

A. one per window
B. two per window
C. three per window
D. four per window

43. All emergency systems switchboards and panelboards shall be provided with _____ protection.

A. AFCI
B. LCDI
C. GFCI
D. surge

44. What is the MINIMUM wire bending space required at the top and bottom of a panelboard that has one (1) size 3/0 AWG conductor connected to each busbar in the panelboard?

A. 6½ inches
B. 8 inches
C. 7½ inches
D. 6 inches

45. Given: A six (6) foot high chain-link fence topped with razor-wire, used to deter access by persons who are not qualified, encloses an outdoor installation of electrical apparatus rated 12 kV. The razor-wire shall be at LEAST_____ in height to comply with the NEC® standards.

A. 24 inches
B. 18 inches
C. 12 inches
D. 6 inches

46. When used as service entrance conductors, size 250 kcmil Type IGS cable has an allowable ampacity of _____.

A. 215 amperes
B. 225 amperes
C. 119 amperes
D. 205 amperes

47. Where a fused disconnect switch is used as the disconnecting means for an air-conditioning unit, the disconnect switch shall have an ampere rating of at LEAST _____ of the nameplate rated-load current of the equipment or branch-circuit selection current, whichever is greater.

A. 100%
B. 115%
C. 150%
D. 175%

48. Metal plugs or plates used to close unused openings in nonmetallic enclosures shall be recessed at LEAST _____ from the outer surface of the enclosure.

A. 1/2 in.
B. 1/8 in.
C. 1/16 in.
D. 1/4 in.

49. In the bedroom of a residence, any wall space having a width of _____ or more (including space measured around corners) and unbroken along the floor line by doorways or similar openings or fixed obstructions shall have a 125-volt, 15- or 20-ampere receptacle installed.

A. 6 feet
B. 10 feet
C. 4 feet
D. 2 feet

50. As a general rule, cables and conductors of Class 2 and Class 3 circuits shall NOT be placed in any _____ with the conductors of electric light and power circuit conductors unless, they are separated by a barrier.

A. device box
B. cable tray
C. manhole
D. device box, cable tray or manhole

51. Given: An induction-type, 3-phase, continuous-duty, ac motor has the following related information marked on the nameplate:

FLA -54 amperes
Temperature rise - 50°C

Your task is to select the initial MAXIMUM size overload devices, in amperes, that is responsive to motor to protect the motor from overload. Assume the value you select will allow the motor and start without tripping and modification of this value is not necessary.

A. 62.1 amperes
B. 67.5 amperes
C. 54.0 amperes
D. 75.6 amperes

52. The connection between the grounded circuit conductor and the equipment grounding conductor at the electrical service is recognized as the _____ in the NEC®.

A. main bonding jumper
B. grounding electrode conductor
C. equipment bonding jumper
D. neutral conductor

53. In guest rooms and guest suites of hotels and motels, at LEAST _____ 125-volt, single-phase, 15- or 20-ampere receptacle(s) is/are required to be readily accessible.

A. one
B. two
C. three
D. four

54. Where a 225-ampere rated panelboard is equipped with snap switches rated for 30-amperes or less, the MAXIMUM overcurrent protection permitted for the panelboard has a rating of

_____.

A. 225 amperes
B. 180 amperes
C. 200 amperes
D. 250 amperes

55. Given: A 3-phase, 480-volt, squirrel-cage, Design B, 50 hp motor has a nameplate FLA rating of 59 amperes. The MAXIMUM initial standard size non-time delay fuses permitted for use as branch-circuit, short-circuit and ground-fault protective devices for the motor is _____.

A. 125 amperes
B. 180 amperes
C. 225 amperes
D. 200 amperes

56. As a general rule, all fixed metal parts such as metal piping, metal fences, and metal awnings in the proximity of a permanently installed swimming pool are required to be bonded. An exception to this rule is when the metal parts are located at a horizontal distance at least greater than _____ from the inside walls of the pool they shall not be required to be bonded to the equipotential bonding grid.

A. 6 feet
B. 10 feet
C. 5 feet
D. 12 feet

57. The rating of a cord-and-plug connected room air-conditioner unit shall NOT exceed _____ where the unit is connected to a single receptacle supplied by a 30-ampere dedicated branch circuit.

A. 24 amperes
B. 20 amperes
C. 30 amperes
D. 15 amperes

58. When exceptions are not a consideration, when attached to a building, final spans of outside overhead conductors, not over 1,000 volts, shall have a clearance of NOT less than ____ from windows designed to be opened, doors, porches balconies, stairs and fire escapes.

A. 2 feet
B. 3 feet
C. 4 feet
D. 5 feet

59. As a general NEC® rule, The MINIMUM size grounded or ungrounded copper or aluminum conductors permitted to be connected in parallel (electrically joined at both ends) is _____.

A. 6 AWG
B. 1 AWG
C. 1/0AWG
D. 2/0 AWG

60. Legally required standby luminaires (unit equipment), provided for legally required standby illumination systems are to be permanently fixed in place however, they are permitted to be cord-and-plug connected provided the flexible cord does NOT exceed _____ in length.

A. 18 inches
B. 2 feet
C. 3 feet
D. 4 feet

61. In regard to electrified track parking spaces, upon loss of the normal power from the local utility company or other electric supply systems, means shall be provided where energy _____.

A. cannot be fed through a TRU
B. can be fed with a two-wire cord
C. can be fed with an ungrounded receptacle
D. cannot be back-fed through the truck supply equipment

62. According to the NEC®, handholes in metal or nonmetallic poles supporting luminaires shall not be required for poles _____ or less in height above finished grade, if the pole is provided with a hinged base.

A. 5 feet
B. 10 feet
C. 15 feet
D. 20 feet

63. A junction box with a flat blank cover and no clamps will contain the following conductors:

- six – size 14 AWG THHN
- eight – size 12 THWN
- three – size 10 THW

The junction box is required to have a volume, in cubic inches, of _____.

A. 24.0 cubic inches
B. 29.5 cubic inches
C. 35.0 cubic inches
D. 37.5 cubic inches

64. A hazardous location where flammable gases, flammable vapors, or combustible liquid-produced vapors may be present in the air in quantities sufficient to produce explosive or ignitible mixtures, is a _____ location.

A. Class I
B. Class II
C. Class III
D. Class IV

65. Determine the MAXIMUM standard size overcurrent protection permitted for a 480-volt transformer having primary full-load current rating of 40 amperes where primary protection only is required.

A. 60 amperes
B. 50 amperes
C. 80 amperes
D. 100 amperes

66. All single-phase, 120-volt, 15- and 20-ampere branch circuits supplying outlets or devices installed in residential kitchens or similar rooms shall be protected by a listed arc-fault circuit-interrupter of the _____ type.

A. individual
B. series connected
C. combination
D. parallel

67. Outdoor installed spas and hot tubs are permitted to be cord-and-plug connected with a flexible cord NOT longer than _____where protected by a ground-fault circuit interrupter.

A. 10 feet
B. 15 feet
C. 8 feet
D. 12 feet

68. Luminaires installed in fountains shall be protected by a ground-fault circuit interrupter and operate at a voltage NOT to exceed _____ between conductors.

A. 150 volts
B. 120 volts
C. 250 volts
D. 25 volts

69. Which of the following is NOT required to be marked on the nameplate of a motor?

A. manufacturer's name
B. full-load current
C. rated temperature rise
D. overcurrent protection

70. What MINIMUM size ungrounded (phase) THWN copper service entrance conductors are required for a 208Y/120-volt, 3-phase commercial service with a demand load of 72,000 VA?

A. 260 kcmil
B. 2/0 AWG
C. 3/0 AWG
D. 4/0 AWG

71. Refer to the previous question and determine the required trade size of rigid metal conduit (RMC) for use as a service riser to enclose the conductors.

A. 2 in.
B. 2½ in.
C. 1½ in.
D. 3 in.

72. The ampacity adjustment factors shown in Table 310.15(B)(3)(a), shall only be required to be applied to conductors in a metal wireway, where the number of current-carrying conductors exceeds _____ at any cross-section of the wireway.

A. 4
B. 20
C. 30
D. 25

73. Every panelboard circuit and circuit modification shall be:

A. marked before installing.
B. legibly identified at the panelboard to its use.
C. copper branch circuit conductors only.
D. a maximum of three (3) 2-pole, 30 ampere branch circuits.

74. Where a vertical raceway contains three (3) size 3/0 AWG copper conductors, the conductors shall be supported at intervals NOT greater
than _____ with an additional support at the top of the conduit run.

A. 80 feet
B. 60 feet
C. 30 feet
D. 40 feet

75. In general, 4 in. wide underfloor raceways shall have a covering of wood or concrete NOT less than _____ above the raceway.

A. 1/2 in.
B. 3/4 in.
C. 1 in.
D. 1¼ in.

76. Branch circuit conductors within 3 inches of a ballast of a fluorescent or HID luminaire shall have an insulation temperature rating of NOT less than _____.

A. 90°F
B. 75°C
C. 110°C
D. 90°C

77. The service conductors between the terminals of the service equipment and a point usually outside the building, clear of building walls, where joined by splice or tap to the service drop or overhead service conductors, are recognized as _____.

A. service lateral conductors
B. service drop conductors
C. service entrance conductors
D. none of these

78. All 15- and 20-ampere, 125-volt and 250-volt nonlocking receptacles located in damp or wet locations shall be a listed _____ type.

A. weather-resistant
B. watertight
C. water-resistant
D. weatherproof

79. In the lubrication pit area of a minor repair commercial garage where ventilation is not provided, the pit below floor level shall be a _____ location that extends up to the floor level.

A. Class I, Division 1
B. Class I, Division 2
C. Class II, Division 1
D. Class II, Division 2

80. What is the MAXIMUM number of times a wire-type grounding electrode conductor is permitted to be spliced by the use of split-bolt connectors?

A. one
B. two
C. three
D. none

81. What is the general lighting demand load on the ungrounded (phase) conductors, in VA, of an industrial commercial (loft) building having dimensions of 100 ft. by 300 ft.

A. 60,000 VA
B. 75,000 VA
C. 90,000 VA
D. 105,000 VA

82. In the critical care (Category 1) spaces of health care facilities, a patient care vicinity shall be permitted to have an optional patient equipment grounding point. An equipment bonding jumper NOT small than _____ shall be used to connect the grounding terminal of all grounding-type receptacles to the patient equipment grounding point.

A. 14 AWG
B. 12 AWG
C. 10 AWG
D. 8 AWG

83. Given: Type UF cable is to be used for direct buried residential branch circuits of 120-volts. The conductors are GFCI protected and overcurrent protection is rated 20-amperes; the UF cable does not cross under any driveways or concrete. What is the MINIMUM required burial depth of the cable?

A. 6 inches
B. 18 inches
C. 24 inches
D. 12 inches

84. _____ is NOT permitted to be installed in theaters and similar locations unless it is encased in concrete.

A. Electrical metallic tubing (EMT)
B. Flexible metal conduit (FMC)
C. Schedule 40 PVC
D. Rigid metal conduit (RMC)

85. When a 240-volt, single-phase residential branch circuit using copper Type NM cable is used to supply an 8-kW rated counter-mounted cooking unit and a wall-mounted oven rated 6 kW, what MINIMUM size NM cable is required?

A. 6/3 AWG with ground
B. 8/3 AWG with ground
C. 4/3 AWG with ground
D. 10/3 AWG with ground

86. The entire area of an aircraft maintenance and storage hangar, including any adjacent and communicating areas not suitably cut off from the hangar, shall be classified as a Class I, Division 2 or Zone 2 location up to a level of _____ above the floor.

A. 18 inches
B. 24 inches
C. 12 inches
D. 30 inches

87. What is the MAXIMUM number of size 4 AWG THHN copper conductors permitted by the NEC® that may be installed in a trade size 1¼ in. electrical metallic tubing (EMT) 18-inch-long nipple?

A. 10
B. 11
C. 12
D. 13

88. Luminaires installed over highly combustible material shall be of the _____ type and located 8 ft. above the floor or guarded.

A. totally enclosed
B. fire-retardant
C. incandescent
D. unswitched

89. Arc-fault circuit protection for 120-volt, single-phase, 15- and 20-ampere branch circuits supplying outlets and devices shall be provided for various areas and rooms in a dwelling. However, which one of the following areas of a dwelling does NOT require AFCI protection for the branch circuits?

A. closets
B. hallways
C. laundry area
D. bathrooms

90. When doing conduit fill calculations, for cables that have elliptical cross-sections, the cross-sectional area calculation shall be based on using the _____ diameter ellipse as a circular diameter.

A. major
B. minor
C. total
D. circular

91. Where circuit breakers are used as switches in 120-volt and 277-volt fluorescent lighting circuits they shall be listed and marked with _____ on the circuit breaker.

I. SWD
II. HID

A. I only
B. II only
C. either I or II
D. both I and II

92. Determine the MINIMUM number of 120-volt, 15-ampere general-lighting branch circuits required for a 15,000 sq. ft. multifamily dwelling unit.

A. 20
B. 25
C. 15
D. 30

93. Wiring located above heated ceilings shall be spaced at not less than 2 inches above the heated ceiling and shall be considered as operating at an ambient temperature of _____.

A. 50°C
B. 86°F
C. 60°C
D. 75°C

94. Unless approved for a higher voltage, surface nonmetallic raceways are NOT approved where the voltage is _____ or more between conductors.

A. 120 volts
B. 150 volts
C. 300 volts
D. 277 volts

95. At marinas and boatyards, the electrical datum plane, in land areas subject to tidal fluctuation, is a horizontal plane _____ above the highest high tide under normal circumstances.

A. 1 foot
B. 2 feet
C. 3 feet
D. 4 feet

96. Given: A feeder circuit using aluminum conductors is installed in PVC conduit and protected by a 500-ampere rated circuit breaker. What is the MINIMUM size aluminum conductor permitted for use as the equipment grounding conductor.

A. 3 AWG
B. 2 AWG
C. 2/0 AWG
D. 1/0 AWG

97. Bends in liquidtight flexible nonmetallic conduit (LFNC) shall be made so that the conduit will not be damaged, and the internal diameter of the conduit will not be reduced. Bends can be made _____.

A. manually without auxiliary equipment
B. with conduit benders specifically identified for the purpose
C. full shoe benders only
D. one shot benders only

98. Where an information technology equipment room houses electronic computer/data processing equipment, the disconnecting means for the equipment shall be:

A. at readily accessible locations in case of fire.
B. locked and protected from unqualified personnel.
C. located as near as practicable to the main service disconnect.
D. not required if the equipment room is provided with a fire suppression
    system.

99. When size 500 kcmil copper conductors with THWN insulation are used as service entrance conductors, the MAXIMUM standard size circuit breaker permitted for use as overcurrent protection has a rating of ____.

A. 350 amperes
B. 400 amperes
C. 375 amperes
D. 300 amperes

100. The disconnecting means for transport refrigerated units (TRUs) located in electrified truck parking spaces of a truck plaza, shall be readily accessible and NOT more than _____ from the receptacle it controls.

A. 36 inches.
B. 24 inches
C. 30 inches
D. 48 inches

Please See Answer Key on following page

ALH 08/07/2019

1Exam Prep
NFPA 70 National Electrical Code, 2017
Final Exam 2
Questions and Answers

ANSWER KEY

Answer	Section/Page#
1. B	310.15(B) (7)
2. A	250.53(B)
3. B	Table 430.248 404.14(A)(3)

15 Ampere switch x 80% = 12 amperes
FLC of motor – 12 amperes x 125% = 15 amperes

Answer	Section/Page#
4. D	240.21(B)(2)(1)
5. D	430.11
6. B	250.94(1)-(6)
7. D	352.20(B)
8. D	312.5(C), Exception
9. B	322.10(1)
10. C	230.95 240.13
11. D	760.130(B)(2)
12. A	430.110(A)
13. B	424.39
14. B	250.66(A)
15. D	408.5
16. A	314.71(A)
17. D	530.14
18. B	392.10(B)(1)(a)

<u>Answer</u>	<u>Section/Page#</u>
19. C	340.10(1)-(4)
	340.12(1)
20. A	Table 220.54
21. B	110.26(A)(3)

6.5 ft. x 12 in. (one foot) = 78 inches

22. D	250.53(H)
23. C	210.19(A)(4), Exception #1(c)
24. B	440.22(A)
25. A	110.26(C)(2)
26. B	352.44
27. D	410.5, Exception
28. C	430.6(A)(1)
	Table 430.250
	430.24(1) &(2)
	Table 310.15(B)(16)

15 hp FLC – 42 amperes x 125% = 52.5 amperes
7½ hp FLC – 22 amperes x 100% = <u>22.0 amperes</u>
74.5 amperes

Size 4 AWG THWN conductors with an ampacity of 85 amperes should be selected from Table 310.15(B)(16).

29. A	404.14(B)(2)
30. A	300.4(A)(2)
31. D	250.6(B)
32. D	547.2
33. D	210.19(A), Info. Note #4
34. C	680.41
35. A	701.12
36. B	Chapter 9, Note 4 to Tables
37. C	605.9(B)

Answer	Section/Page#
38 A.	240.51(B)
39. D	513.3(B)
40. B	Table 110.26(A)(1)
41. D	645.10(B)(3) & (4)
42. B	210.62

One receptacle is required for each 12 ft. of show window or major fraction thereof. Therefore, two receptacles are required for each 15 ft. of show window.

43. D	700.8
44. A	Table 312.6(B), Column 1
45. C	110.31
46. C	Table 326.80
47. B	440.12(A)(1)
48. D	110.12(A)
49. D	210.52(A)(2)(1)
50. D	725.136(A)
51. A	430.32(A)(1)

FLA of motor – 54 amperes x 115% = 62.1 amperes

52. A	Article 100 – Definitions
53. B	210.60(B)
54. C	408.36(A)
55. D	430.6(A)
	Table 430.250
	Table 430.52
	430.52(C)(1), Exception 1
	Table 240.6(A)

FLC of motor – 65 amperes x 300% = 195 amperes
The next standard size non-time delay fuses are rated 200 amperes.

56. C	680.26(B)(7), Exception 2

Answer	Section/Page#
57. A	440.62(B)

30 amperes x 80% = 24 amperes

58. B	225.19(D)(1)
59. C	310.10(H)(1)
60. C	701.12(G)
61. D	626.26
62. D	410.30(B)(1), Exception 2
63. D	Table 314.16(B)

Size 14 AWG – 6 wires x 2.00 cu. in. = 12.0 cu. in.
Size 12 AWG - 8 wires x 2.25 cu. in. = 18.0 cu. in.
Size 10 AWG - 3 wires x 2.50 cu. in. = 7.5 cu. in.
Total = 37.5 Cu. in.

64. A	500.5(B)
65. B	450.3(B) Table 450.3(B) Table 240.6(A)

Primary current – 40 amperes x 125% = 50 amperes

66. C	210.12(A)(1)
67. B	680.42(A)(2)
68. A	680.51(B)
69. D	430.7(A)(1)-(5)
70. C	3-phase current formula Table 310.15(B)(16)

$$I = P \div E \times 1.732 \quad I = \frac{72,000 \text{ VA}}{208 \times 1.732} = \frac{72,000}{360.25} = 199.8 \text{ amperes}$$

Size 3/0 AWG THWN conductors with an allowable ampacity of 200 amperes should be selected.

71. A	Annex C, Table C.9
72. C	376.22(B)

Answer	Section/Page#
73. B	408.4(A)
74. A	Table 300.19(A)
75. B	390.4(A)
76. D	410.68
77. C	Article 100 – Definitions
78. A	406.9(A)
79. B	Table 511.3(C)
80. D	250.64(C)
81. B	Table 220.12 Article 100 – Definitions 230.42(A)(1)

100 ft. x 300 ft. = 30,000 sq. ft. x 2 VA = 60,000 VA
60,000 VA x 125% (continuous load) = 75,000 VA

82. C	517.19(D)
83. D	Table 300.5, Column 4
84. C	520.5(A)
85. B	334.80 Table 220.55, Notes 1 & 2 Single-phase current formula Table 310.15(B)(16)

8 kW + 6 kW = 14 kW (treat as one range)
14 kW – 12 kW = 2 kW x 5% = 10% increase in column C
8 kW (column C) x 110% = 8.8 kW

$$I = P \div E \quad I = \frac{8.8 \text{ kW x } 1000}{240 \text{ volts}} = \frac{8800}{240} = 36.7 \text{ amperes}$$

Size 8 AWG conductors with an ampacity of 40 amperes should be selected from the 60°C column of Table 310.15(B)(16).

86. A	513.3(B)

Answer	Section/Page#

87. B

Chapter 9, Table 4
Chapter 9, Table 5
Note 7 to Chapter 9 Tables

$$\frac{0.897 \text{ sq. in (conduit)}}{0.0824 \text{ sq. in. (wire)}} = 10.8 = 11 \text{ wires}$$

88. D   410.12

89. D   210.12(A)

90. A   Chapter 9, Note 9 to Tables

91. C   240.83(D)

92. B   Table 220.12

15,000 sq. ft. x 3 VA = 45,000 VA (load)
120 volts x 15 amperes = 1,800 VA (one circuit)

$$\frac{45,000 \text{ VA (load)}}{1,800 \text{ VA (1 ckt.)}} = 25 \text{ (15 ampere general lighting circuits)}$$

93. A   424.36

94. C   388.12(3)

95. B   555.2(1)

96. D   Table 250.122

97. A   356.24

98. A   645.10(A)(1)

99. B   Table 310.15(B)(16)
240.4(B)
Table 240.6(A)

100. C   626.31(B)

Ugly's Electrical Reference
Questions

1. A _____ KW, _____ V direct-current generator is used to power a variable-speed conveyor belt at a rock-crushing plant.

    A. 60, 100
    B. 45, 140
    C. 75, 240
    D. 55, 200

2. Branch Circuit Conductors use _____ percent of full-load current to find conductor size.

    A. 140
    B. 100
    C. 200
    D. 125

3. To change rotation direction of _____ phase motor, swap any two T-leads.

    A. 4
    B. 2
    C. 3
    D. 6

4. U.L. listed transformers 25KVA and larger have a +/- _____ percent impedance tolerance. Short-circuit amperes can be affected by this tolerance.

    A. 25
    B. 15
    C. 10
    D. 22

5. The _____ KW unit heater cannot be balanced across all three phases.

    A. 8
    B. 10
    C. 3
    D. 5

6. A 150-ampere circuit breaker is labeled for _____ C terminations and is selected to be used for a 150-ampere, noncontinuous load.

     A. 63
     B. 82
     C. 75
     D. 90

7. For ranges individually rated more than 12 KW but not more than 27 kW, the maximum demand in Column C shall be increased _____ percent for each additional kilowatt of rating or major fraction thereof by which the rating of individual ranges exceeds _____ kW.

     A. 10, 20
     B. 8, 10
     C. 5, 12
     D. 25, 15

8. A 100-watt incandescent lamp is to be replaced with a _____ watt, energy saving lamp that has the same light output (lumens).

     A. 40
     B. 26
     C. 32
     D. 15

9. Community solar installations and brownfield solar installations are often large-scale PV systems that are in excess of _____ Mw each.

     A. 5
     B. 10
     C. 25
     D. 12

10. Tamper-resistant receptacles requirements are applicable to _____ and _____ volt receptacles and were expanded to include mobile homes and manufactured homes, preschool and elementary educational facilities, dormitories, business offices, corridors, waiting rooms, gymnasiums, skating rinks, and other occupancies.

     A. 125, 250
     B. 200, 220
     C. 130, 160
     D. 100, 240

11. There are _____ appliances that are required to have GFCI protection for personnel throughout Article 422.

    A. 3
    B. 8
    C. 5
    D. 10

12. A 230-V, single-phase circuit has a _____ KW power load, and operates at _____ percent power factor.

    A. 12, 84
    B. 15, 65
    C. 20, 80
    D. 10, 70

13. Circumference of a Circle is _____ x _____ x radius.

    A. 2.14, 6
    B. 3.14, 4
    C. 1.14, 2
    D. 3.1416, 2

14. ARC Length equals degrees in arc x radius x _____.

    A. 1.254
    B. 1.1745
    C. 0.01745
    D. 0.0234

15. Sector is a part of a circle enclosed by _____ radii and the arc that they cut off.

    A. four
    B. three
    C. one
    D. two

16. A Triangle is a figure enclosed by _____ straight sides.

    A. two
    B. six
    C. four
    D. three

17. Right Triangles are triangles that have one angle of ____ degrees and two angles of less than ____ degrees.

    A. 90, 90
    B. 90, 65
    C. 50, 90
    D. 70, 90

18. To help you remember the ____ trigonometric functions, memorize, Oh Hell Another Hour of Andy.

    A. three
    B. six
    C. ten
    D. five

19. To make a fifteen inch offset, using thirty degree bends, multiply ____ times the offset desired.

    A. three
    B. two
    C. six
    D. four

20. To determine how much offset is needed to make a rolling offset, measure ____ degrees from the vertical line measurement and mark.

    A. 75
    B. 45
    C. 30
    D. 90

21. The shrink constant for ____ degrees is 3/8 inches.

    A. 12
    B. 45
    C. 30
    D. 25

22. The Multiplier for 50 degrees is ____.

    A. 8
    B. 1.3
    C. 1
    D. 2.2

23. A 12-volt motor draws a current of _____ amperes and has an efficiency rating of _____ percent.

    A. 5.3, 83
    B. 9.2, 89
    C. 7.6, 77
    D. 8.09, 96

24. If putting a 40 degrees bend in 3/4 inches conduit, the bend length is _____ inches.

    A. 5
    B. 2
    C. 3
    D. 4

25. D is the deduct for whatever size conduit is being run. This formula works for any angle between _____ and _____ degrees.

    A. 120, 360
    B. 0, 90
    C. 90, 120
    D. 45, 120

26. To determine the Take-Up and Shrink of each size conduit for a particular bender to make _____ degree lends use a straight piece of scrap conduit.

    A. 20
    B. 90
    C. 120
    D. 45

27. To bend a 6 inch offset, make a mark of _____ inches from the conduit end.

    A. 3
    B. 6
    C. 5
    D. 8

28. When dealing with layout and bending, on all three conduit, point B will be _____ inches from point A.

    A. 10
    B. 15
    C. 18.75
    D. 20.2

29. On all three conduit, point C will be _____ inches from point D.

     A. 15.2
     B. 30.75
     C. 21.3
     D. 25

30. Spaces should not be more than _____ inches to prevent wrinkling of the conduit.

     A. 15
     B. 1.75
     C. 2
     D. 3.2

31. When determining the number of shots, choose a number that will divide into _____ an even number of times.

     A. ninety
     B. fifty
     C. one hundred
     D. eighty

32. When using a hand bender, align the arrow on bender with the last mark made on the EMT, and bend to the _____ degree mark on the bender.

     A. 30
     B. 80
     C. 45
     D. 90

33. The _____ point saddle bend is used when encountering an obstacle.

     A. 8
     B. 3
     C. 6
     D. 5

34. A single-phase, 115-volt ac motor has an efficiency rating of _____ percent and a power factor of _____ percent.

     A. 86, 94
     B. 62, 43
     C. 75, 56
     D. 92, 80

35. When using a hand bender, multiply the height of the obstruction by _____ and mark this distance on each side of the center mark.

    A. 2.5
    B. 3.2
    C. 1.8
    D. 5.4

36. When using a hand bender, place the center mark on the saddle mark or notch. Bend to _____ degree.

    A. 45
    B. 50
    C. 90
    D. 65

37. The distance between energized conductors or between energized conductors and ground. Shorter arc gaps result in less energy being expended in the arc, while longer gaps reduce arc current. For _____ volts and below, arc gaps of _____ inches typically produce the maximum incident energy.

    A. 120, 5.2
    B. 600, 1.25
    C. 700, 1.5
    D. 240, 2.3

38. Distance to arc refers to the distance from the receiving surface to the arc center. The value used for most calculations is typically _____ inches.

    A. 7
    B. 10
    C. 9
    D. 18

39. A prime-rated engine is rated to deliver a continuous output with approximately _____ percent reserved for surges.

    A. 15
    B. 35
    C. 10
    D. 23

40. Microturbines range in size from ____ to ____ KW and are modular. They can operate on a wide variety of fuels but are only considered as a renewable energy source.

     A. 40, 70
     B. 25, 500
     C. 300, 600
     D. 50, 100

41. To perform CPR give ____ chest compressions at a rate of at least ____ compressions per minute, allowing the chest to return to its normal position after each compression.

     A. 40, 100
     B. 30, 100
     C. 20, 80
     D. 50, 200

42. _____ are protection boundaries established to protect personnel from shock.

     A. Exposed Live Part
     B. Arc Gap
     C. Approach Boundaries
     D. Flame Resistant

43. _____ is trauma subjected to the body by electrical current. When personnel come in contact with energized conductors, it can result in current flowing through their body often causing serious injury or death.

     A. PPE
     B. Incident Energy
     C. Flash Suit
     D. Shock

44. ____ is a term referring to a complete FR rated Personal Protective Equipment (PPE) system that would cover a persons body, excluding the hands and feet. Included would be pants, shirt/jacket, and flash hood with a built-in face shield.

     A. Shock
     B. Flash Suit
     C. Calorie
     D. PPE

45. A three-phase, 460-volt motor draws a current of _____ amperes.

    A. 86
    B. 52
    C. 64
    D. 70

46. NFPA 70E Article _____ contains detailed instructions for lockout/tagout and placing equipment in an Electrically Safe Work Condition.

    A. 90
    B. 100
    C. 120
    D. 75

47. One horsepower is the amount of energy required to lift _____ pounds, 1 foot, in 1 minute.

    A. 40,000
    B. 33,000
    C. 15,000
    D. 25,000

48. One watt is the amount of energy required to lift _____ pounds, 1 foot, in 1 minute.

    A. 44.26
    B. 50.23
    C. 63.32
    D. 70.2

49. A three-phase, _____ volt generator delivers 52 amperes.

    A. 240
    B. 500
    C. 320
    D. 460

50. The size capacitor needed to equal the motors stored reactive power is _____ KVAR.

    A. 6
    B. 3
    C. 5
    D. 8

Ugly's Electrical Reference
Answers

1.	C	26.	B
2.	D	27.	A
3.	C	28.	C
4.	C	29.	B
5.	D	30.	B
6.	C	31.	A
7.	C	32.	D
8.	B	33.	B
9.	A	34.	D
10.	A	35.	A
11.	C	36.	A
12.	A	37.	B
13.	D	38.	D
14.	C	39.	C
15.	D	40.	B
16.	D	41.	B
17.	A	42.	C
18.	B	43.	D
19.	B	44.	B
20.	D	45.	B
21.	B	46.	C
22.	B	47.	B
23.	D	48.	A
24.	D	49.	D
25.	B	50.	A

Made in United States
Orlando, FL
13 November 2024